K-9 Police Units

Other titles in Lucent's Crime Scene Investigations series include:

K-9 Police Units

by Gail B. Stewart

LUCENT BOOKS
A part of Gale, Cengage Learning

GALE
CENGAGE Learning

Detroit • New York • San Francisco • New Haven, Conn • Waterville, Maine • London

GALE
CENGAGE Learning™

LIBRARY OF CONGRESS CATALOGING-IN-PUBLICATION DATA

Stewart, Gail B. (Gail Barbara), 1949-
  K-9 police units / by Gail B. Stewart.
     p. cm. -- (Crime scene investigations)
  Includes bibliographical references and index.
  ISBN 978-1-4205-0137-7 (hbk.)
  1. Police dogs--Juvenile literature. I. Title.
  HV8025.S74 2010
  363.28--dc22
                                                         2009027456

Lucent Books
27500 Drake Rd.
Farmington Hills, MI 48331

ISBN-13: 978-1-4205-0137-7
ISBN-10: 1-4205-0137-2

Printed in the United States of America
1 2 3 4 5 6 7 13 12 11 10 09

Printed by Bang Printing, Brainerd, MN, 1st Ptg., 10/2009

Contents

Foreword

The popularity of crime scene and investigative crime shows on television has come as a surprise to many who work in the field. The main surprise is the concept that crime scene analysts are the true crime solvers, when in truth, it takes dozens of people, doing many different jobs, to solve a crime. Often, the crime scene analyst's contribution is a small one. One Minnesota forensic scientist says that the public "has gotten the wrong idea. Because I work in a lab similar to the ones on *CSI*, people seem to think I'm solving crimes left and right—just me and my microscope. They don't believe me when I tell them that it's the investigators that are solving crimes, not me."

Crime scene analysts do have an important role to play, however. Science has rapidly added a whole new dimension to gathering and assessing evidence. Modern crime labs can match a hair of a murder suspect to one found on a murder victim, for example, or recover a latent fingerprint from a threatening letter, or use a powerful microscope to match tool marks made during the wiring of an explosive device to a tool in a suspect's possession.

Probably the most exciting of the forensic scientist's tools is DNA analysis. DNA can be found in just one drop of blood, a dribble of saliva on a toothbrush, or even the residue from a fingerprint. Some DNA analysis techniques enable scientists to tell with certainty, for example, whether a drop of blood on a suspect's shirt is that of a murder victim.

While these exciting techniques are now an essential part of many investigations, they cannot solve crimes alone. "DNA doesn't come with a name and address on it," says the Minnesota forensic scientist. "It's great if you have someone in custody to match the sample to, but otherwise, it doesn't help. That's the investigator's job. We can have all the great DNA evidence in the world, and without a suspect, it will just sit on the shelf. We've all seen cases with very little forensic evidence get solved by the resourcefulness of a detective."

While forensic specialists get the most media attention today, the work of detectives still forms the core of most criminal investigations. Their job, in many ways, has changed little over the years. Most cases are still solved through the persistence and determination of a criminal detective whose work may be anything but glamorous. Many cases require routine, even mind-numbing tasks. After the July 2005 bombings in London, for example, police officers sat in front of video players watching thousands of hours of closed-circuit television tape from security cameras throughout the city, and as a result were able to get the first images of the bombers.

The Lucent Books Crime Scene Investigations series explores the variety of ways crimes are solved. Titles cover particular crimes such as murder, specific cases such as the killing of three civil rights workers in Mississippi, or the role specialists such as medical examiners play in solving crimes. Each title in the series demonstrates the ways a crime may be solved, from the various applications of forensic science and technology to the reasoning of investigators. Sidebars examine both the limits and possibilities of the new technologies and present crime statistics, career information, and step-by-step explanations of scientific and legal processes.

The Crime Scene Investigations series strives to be both informative and realistic about how members of law enforcement—criminal investigators, forensic scientists, and others—solve crimes, for it is essential that student researchers understand that crime solving is rarely quick or easy. Many factors—from a detective's dogged pursuit of one tenuous lead to a suspect's careless mistakes to sheer luck to complex calculations computed in the lab—are all part of crime solving today.

"It's Absolutely Unbelievable"

It was a hot summer day when Albany County, Wyoming, sheriff's deputy Cathy Orde received a call about a lost child. A two-year-old boy had wandered away from his parents' trailer in the Sierra Madre range. He had been gone for hours, and even with the help of police officers and other volunteers, not a single clue had been found. Because Orde had a seven-year-old golden retriever, Moose, who was good at tracking lost people, local police requested that she and Moose come as quickly as possible.

"I Was Practically Airborne"

When she arrived, the distraught parents gave her an article of the child's clothing so Moose would know the scent he would be tracking. Orde asked for support from a searcher who was in good physical shape to accompany her as she worked Moose. After circling the trailer Moose found a fresh scent and, nose to the ground, led Orde and the support searcher downhill through the forest.

Orde later recalled that the searcher was skeptical about Moose's chances of finding the boy. "[He] kept saying, 'A two-year-old won't go downhill, and they won't go this far!'" But as they went on behind the dog, Orde began to spot some very small footprints in the pine needles. Then Moose began running, and Orde quickly unhooked the lead. "I was practically airborne,"[1] she remembers.

Just before she and the searcher came to an area of tall brush into which Moose had disappeared, the dog came running back to her with a little baseball cap in his mouth. Orde gave the command "show me," and the dog led her to the boy. "I made sure he was okay," she said, "picked him up in my arms, and hugged him. I told him I was taking him back to his mommy. . . . As I carried the little boy out of the forest, Moose stayed close by us, bouncing up and down."[2] It had taken Moose a total of thirty-five minutes to find the boy, who had walked over a mile (1.6km) from his home.

Justice Done

In another case Philadelphia police got a call that gunshots had just been fired in the city's twenty-fifth police district. When officers arrived they saw three young men running through a field and heard a gunshot. The officers then chased the man who had fired the gun. They caught him, but although he had a single .38 caliber round in his pocket, he had evidently thrown the gun away to avoid being arrested. Without a gun it would be impossible to prove his guilt.

After searching for forty-five minutes in the dark and finding no sign of the gun, police called for Officer John Callahan and his dog Justice to help recover the weapon. It took them five minutes from the time they arrived on the scene for Justice to show Callahan that he had found the weapon—a powerful .357 Magnum—with one spent shell. With DNA and fingerprint analysis of the weapon, it would be possible to tie the suspect to it.

"That's *Exactly* What We Want"

Almost 1,000 miles (1,609km) away from Philadelphia, St. Paul police officer Mike Ernster received a radio message from dispatch. Witnesses had seen a man fire a gun from a white Ford Expedition SUV, and the vehicle was heading Ernster's way. Within a few minutes Ernster spotted the car and signaled with his lights for the driver to pull over.

Ernster knew very well that this was a difficult situation. Someone in the car had already pulled the trigger of a gun, and the officer had no way of knowing whether he would be the

A police K-9 officer restrains his dog while a suspect is taken into custody. The presence of the dog often convinces criminals to surrender rather than fight it out with police.

next target. Getting out of his car, he grabbed a long leather lead and snapped it on the collar of his police dog, Buzz, who was sitting in the back of the squad car.

The situation defused almost as quickly as it began. Ernster stood back by his car, holding Buzz's lead while shouting for the driver to get out with his hands up. Buzz was straining against the lead and barking loudly, hoping to be released, but Ernster held him tight. With a nervous look toward the dog, the driver obeyed and walked backward toward the police car with his hands up. Within a few seconds another squad car arrived, and the officer helped arrest each of the men in the SUV.

Though Buzz did not apprehend the suspect, both Ernster and the other officer knew that the dog's role was huge. Without Buzz it might easily have been a much different situation. "That's *exactly* what we want," said Ernster. "[Suspects] do not want to run, to fight, or to cause any problems because the dog is there. The dog is a deterrent."[3]

"The Coolest Thing Ever"

Cases like these happen every day. A felon flees from police, someone becomes lost in a remote area, and criminals try to smuggle dangerous drugs across the border into the United States. And in these and dozens of other situations, police and other law enforcement agencies are turning to K-9 teams. (*K-9* is short for *canine*, another word for *dog*.) As of 2008 more than eighteen hundred K-9 teams were being used to track and apprehend criminals, sniff out illegal materials, search buildings, locate the bodies of victims of crimes or natural disasters, and do other jobs that police cannot do as well as a dog can.

The working relationship that develops between the dog and its partner—through intensive training and lots of experience—can yield impressive results in terms of fighting crime. K-9 work is not random, but rather works on systems that are constantly being evaluated, tested, and revised by trainers. At its core, however, successful K-9 work relies on trust and communication

"You protect each other—Kodiak and I are partners," explains Officer Kevin Rofidal. *"We're there for each other."* between the dog and handler. And when it works, admits St. Paul K-9 officer Brady Harrison, "It's absolutely unbelievable—the coolest thing ever."[4]

CHAPTER ONE

The K-9 Team

Forming an effective K-9 team starts with selecting the right dog. Police dog trainers say that deciding what breed of dog to choose depends on how the K-9 will be used. Many breeds can be trained successfully to do what is known as "single-purpose" detection work. These are the dogs that can alert a handler to the presence of weapons, drugs, explosives, or even human stowaways trying to cross borders illegally.

The most common breeds used for single-purpose work are Labrador retrievers, spaniels, and beagles—though many mixed-breed dogs are used in detection work, too. Size and strength are fairly unimportant, says trainer Glenn Olson. "It's the nose that does all the work,"[5] he says. In fact, the Geauga County, Ohio, Sheriff's Department boasts the nation's smallest narcotics dog—an 8-pound (3.6kg) Chihuahua named Midge.

However, in patrol work, where a dog will be expected to do a number of jobs—not the least of which is to apprehend criminals—the breed used most often is the German shepherd. According to Olson, there is a good reason for this breed's popularity. "For many generations these have been the dogs used most throughout the world," he says. "They're amazingly smart and very loyal to their handlers. They've got a strong hunting drive to follow the scent of a suspect. And they can be aggressive when they need to be, but at the end of a shift, they go home and can fit right in with the handler's family."[6]

Four-Legged Imports

But breed alone is not enough. In fact, a great deal of work goes into selecting the dog that will be physically and temperamentally

K-9s and Gender

Almost all K-9s chosen for use by police patrol officers are male. Experts say that female dogs tend to be overprotective of their handlers. During a chase, for example, a female K-9 might be tempted to return to check on her handler, rather than stay on the track of the suspect. On the other hand, female and male dogs are both used for single-purpose scent work, such as sniffing out narcotics or explosives.

strong enough to be part of a K-9 team. In years past, police would get donated dogs and train them for K-9 work; however, today that has changed. Training has become so specialized for modern police work that the demand for better dogs has resulted in many departments—especially those in large cities—importing dogs from Europe. Says St. Paul K-9 trainer Mark Ficcadenti:

> It doesn't mean that there aren't good breeders here in America. There certainly are. But those good American breeders don't produce enough quality dogs. And because we train handlers not only from our department, but from lots of other places, we need to order usually between 12 and 18 dogs each year—in fact, one year we ordered 39. There was no way we could get that many quality dogs here in the United States, at least as things are right now.[7]

Minneapolis K-9 trainer Andy Stender agrees, adding that he worries about the overbreeding that is done by breeders in the United States. He says: "With many of the American breeders there is a lot of inbreeding—breeding the same dogs too often—and that can create physical problems. You see a

lot more genetic problems with hips and elbows. Those dogs won't be able to handle all the jumping and running K-9s need to do."[8]

Like many K-9s in the United States, this dog has been imported from an European breeder.

"Now There's a Cool Dog"

But not every dog—no matter how strong its police dog bloodlines—is cut out to be a K-9. Importers or police trainers evaluate the breeders' puppies to see which ones have possibilities. They look at the physical health of the dogs, often making sure with X-rays that the dogs do not have genetic weaknesses in their joints that could lead to problems later on. They look for signs of skin problems in the dogs' ears and coats. One thing they do not necessarily care about is choosing the biggest puppy of

Police K-9s have to be social in addition to helping apprehend criminals. Here an officer explains to children how he has trained his dog.

a litter. In fact, a dog that is far bigger than its littermates can be at a disadvantage on the job, says Tacoma, Washington, K-9 expert Bruce Jackson. "A lot of people think bigger is better [for a puppy], but that's not true," he says. "Big is clumsy. Big is slow. Big lacks agility. Big has a hard time leaping off your back onto a twelve-foot-high roof during a chase."[9]

But there is more to evaluate than physical health. Trainers want dogs that are not aggressive toward other animals and who can be social with all people. They also look for a dog that is curious. "I used to kind of jangle my car keys real loud when I went into an area with a bunch of puppies," says Glenn Olson. "The one who is startled or kind of scared of the noise, or who backs away, isn't the one I want. I want the little guy who says to himself, 'What the heck is that?' and walks over to investigate."[10]

For New Orleans K-9 officer Randy Lewis, the deciding factor in his choice was playfulness. Since almost all of the training K-9s do is treated as a game, it was important to find a dog that enjoyed that interaction with a human—and Lewis found one. "We went to select dogs for training, and this little guy came up and bit me. He looked up and started wagging his tail, but when I didn't react, he kept nipping at me. I thought, 'Now there's a cool dog.'"[11]

"I Told Him I Wasn't Really Interested"

Whatever criteria are used for evaluation, trainers or importers can still be wrong about a dog. That was the case with Minneapolis K-9 trainer Andy Stender and his dog Harley. Stender had flown to the Netherlands to choose a new dog and, during the first days there, was not finding what he was looking for. "At that point, I was thinking that I might be going to go back to Minneapolis without a dog,"[12] recalls Stender.

One of the breeders whose dogs he had looked at suggested he take a second look at one particular dog—a Belgian Malinois puppy (similar to a German shepherd, but a little smaller) that had not impressed Stender at all. However, the breeder insisted that the dog was smart and had a lot of possibilities. "I'd seen him the first time, and he didn't react to me at all," Stender says. "In fact, he just kind of lay there, keeping his distance. So when the breeder told me to give that dog a second look, I told him I wasn't really interested."[13]

But then, Stender says, the breeder told him a story that made him rethink the

By the Numbers

$7,500

Average cost of an imported police K-9 in 2008

Minneapolis K-9 officer Andy Stender and his dog Harley work patrol and also serve on the city's SWAT team.

puppy. He had actually been sold some time before, but the owner came home recently and his wife told him that the dog had bitten her. Furious, the man went out and put on a bite suit—a strong, reinforced garment used in training that can protect against the strongest dog bites. "And then the guy proceeded to basically beat the dog within an inch of his life," says Stender. "After that, he returned the dog to the breeder—said

he didn't want him. That was the day before I'd seen the dog for the first time."[14]

Stender understood that the dog had not been disinterested when he had first seen him. Rather, he was frightened and in pain. Figuring that with good training and a lot of patience the dog could become more confident, Stender decided to trust the breeder and take a chance on the dog, which he named Harley. "I'm really glad I did," he says. "That was nine years ago, and Harley has turned into one amazing dog."[15]

The Demands of a Handler

Once the dogs have been shipped to the United States, they are brought to the police department training facility. The trainer will then assign each young dog to its handler—the officer who will likely be the dog's partner for the next eight to ten years, the average working life span of a K-9. Trainers insist that the human half of the K-9 team needs to be chosen with the same amount of care as the dog. The most intelligent, courageous dog in the world, they say, will be limited if the handler is not able to work and communicate with it.

One important qualification for a handler is being in excellent physical shape. The K-9 who is tracking a dangerous suspect has no trouble keeping up, since police dogs are more than capable of moving fast for hours at a time. But the dog's speed and endurance mean nothing if there is no one on the other end of the lead. Handler Brady Harrison knows very well how exhausting K-9 work can be. He explains:

> You're going over fences in backyards, sometimes having to lift your dog over obstacles that he can't get over on his own. Depending on where you're tracking, you might be going through overgrown areas at night, in snow, wherever. You might be chasing a bad guy up and down hills or flights of stairs—it's really wherever the dog is leading you. It's very challenging physically, because you've got to keep up.[16]

Keeping up with an energetic police K-9 requires officers to stay in top shape.

Besides needing to be very physically fit, prospective handlers need to understand a basic fact of life for K-9 teams: They will be in more dangerous situations on a regular basis than other officers, just by the nature of the job. "K-9 handlers are out front, working point," says Mark Ficcadenti.

> Every time you bring that dog out of the car, he's bringing you for the most part into harm's way. You're asking him to follow the bad guy, to trace someone who might have just shot someone, killed someone. And you're telling the dog, "Find him." Just having that dog means you're always walking into very dangerous situations. And you are the one right behind [the dog], on the other end of the leash. It takes a tactically-minded officer to want to do that.[17]

Training Day

Once handlers and dogs are chosen and are assigned to one another, they go through an intense training regimen that usually lasts between ten and twelve weeks. The training is the first opportunity the handlers have to get to know their dogs and become comfortable with them. The trainer is responsible for teaching the handlers, but all instruction to the dogs comes from the handlers themselves. That way, there is no confusion about who is the dog's pack leader.

The dogs learn obedience commands such as "sit," "come," and "stay," and they must respond quickly. When a handler gives the command to come, the dog must stop whatever it is doing, return to its handler, and plop down on the ground next to him or her. Dogs must also learn "find him" or "seek"—the commands given when the handler wants the dog to use its superior sense of smell to track a suspect who has fled the scene. Dogs must also learn to

By the Numbers

1,000 TO 10,000

How many times keener a dog's sense of smell is than a human's

respond to hand signals by the handler. In cases where police are staking out a suspect and do not want their presence known before making the arrest, the handler needs to be able to communicate silently with the dog, telling it to sit or stay.

In a few police departments, handlers are encouraged to use commands in the language of the dog's native country. The theory is that the dogs have heard the language before, so it is

One of the things K-9s learn is to jump over fences, walls, and other obstacles.

easier for the handler to learn a few foreign commands than it is for the dogs to learn English words. However, most trainers dismiss foreign commands as unnecessary, saying that the dogs quickly learn the commands they need to know.

"Plus, when human beings are under stress, they revert to their native language," says Ficcadenti. "If you're a handler, and you're injured or things are happening in a situation very quickly and you need to communicate with your dog, you may not have the recall of a Dutch or Czech command for your dog."[18]

"That's What We Train For"

The training classes also include agility training, during which dogs become used to doing things that may at first be uncomfortable or scary to them—but which they will encounter on the job. On what is basically an obstacle course, K-9s learn to walk on various surfaces such as slippery floors, open stairs (such as those on an outside fire escape), and grated walkways, where the ground is visible through the metal. They learn to jump through the window of a squad car on command and crawl into plastic tubes that are barely large enough for them to pass through.

"It's all necessary," says Ficcadenti. "Take the last thing, crawling into tight spaces. Dogs are typically afraid of going into dark confined spaces, just like human beings are. But an officer often needs the dog to go into an attic, or a little crawl space—something like that, looking either for a suspect hiding, or a weapon maybe. So a dog needs to be able to get past that fear and do it. So that's what we train for."[19]

Trainers say that the work they do with handlers and dogs is a way of building confidence. But the dogs are not the only ones who become more confident as they get past their fears during training. The handlers, too, become more confident in their dogs. St. Paul K-9 officer Mike Davis, who has a young dog named Auggie, says, "This type of training we do, it builds up confidence in me, watching my dog do this stuff and seeing him get better and better."[20]

Though it is an uncomfortable feeling at first, climbing stairs at such a steep angle is a valuable skill when a K-9 must climb up into an attic to search for a suspect.

The Bite

The most physical—and potentially the most dangerous—of the training exercises teaches dogs to apprehend a suspect who runs away or who refuses to comply with officers at the scene. Police K-9s are trained to chase down and hold suspects by biting them on the arm and holding them fast. Not until the officers approach and see that the suspect is not armed or trying to conceal any dangerous weapon is the command "out" given—the signal that the dog must quickly let go.

To practice this, a decoy (usually the trainer or another K-9 handler) stands in an open area waving a large, menacing-looking stick. The dog stands next to its handler as the officer yells out instructions to the decoy. The officer orders the "suspect" to drop the weapon. The officer tells the suspect to lie down on the ground and warns that if he or she does not, the dog will be released. The decoy refuses again—a situation that happens, say

St. Paul K-9 officer Jason Brodt plays decoy, teaching a dog to bite and hold. At first this is hard for young dogs, because attacking a human goes against their nature.

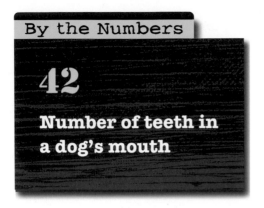

police, all too frequently in real life. At that point the handler gives the signal to the dog to apprehend the decoy.

The decoy is using a special, reinforced, burlap-covered "bite sleeve" that looks like a thick, oversized cast. Bite sleeves will keep decoys from actually being bitten, although each decoy will still experience the sensation of a large 80- to 90-pound (36 to 40kg) dog leaping up and clamping its powerful jaws around his or her arm. Those who have taken their turn at being a decoy say that they feel a pinch, rather than the full effect of the dog's bite.

Making It Real

Though the arm is the preferred target for a K-9 apprehension, a good police dog will hold another part of the body if necessary. For instance, if a dog cannot get a good hold on the right arm, it will go for the other arm, a leg—even the suspect's back. Which arm or leg the K-9 grabs is less important than how well it can hold the suspect on the ground until the handler arrives.

Trainer Mark Ficcadenti says new K-9 handlers are sometimes critical of their dogs for bypassing the bite sleeve and taking hold of another part of the decoy's body. "That's hard for officers, whose first impulse is to scold the dog, get mad," he says. "The appropriate response when your dog releases a bite and takes another part of the body isn't 'No.' It's 'Good boy, good boy!' On the street, you want him to do that if he has to, if [the right arm] isn't easy for him to get to, for example."[21]

Dog handler Harrison Forbes is convinced that sometimes the training is at fault, making dogs nervous about apprehending a real-life suspect. He believes that too many police departments focus just on working with a bite sleeve—something the K-9 will never see an actual suspect wearing. "They'd get out on

K-9s need to learn to hold a bite on another part of the body if the arm is inaccessible. Here a dog in training learns to hold a leg bite on a heavily padded decoy.

the street where lives were at risk," he says, "and the dogs would run up to somebody and be looking for the protective sleeve. . . . When they didn't see it, they would just stand there and bark."[22]

Many trainers vary the apprehension exercise. Sometimes the decoy wears an entire bite suit, so dogs can bite him or her on the legs or back without too much risk of injury. Another choice is to make the decoy look like a normal person, without any bite padding at all. In this case the handler puts a muzzle on the dog, so the K-9 must rely on pushing the suspect down with its snout and standing over him or her until the handler arrives. To give the dog the feeling that it is being successful, the decoy is instructed to fall to the ground the minute the dog hits him or her with its muzzled snout. That will ensure that the dog knows its jaws will always be an important part of the apprehension.

Confronting a human being by biting is not natural for a dog, experts say, but it is very important that the dog learn to do it, since it is a huge part of police work. "We want these dogs to be confident, to stay committed to the bite," says Ficcadenti, "no matter how hard the bad guy fights, no matter how aggressive he is toward the dog. That's part of the K-9's job. And hopefully, the idea of getting chased down by the K-9 is so scary that the bad guy will think twice about running away, or not heeding the police officer's warning."[23]

Nothing but Praise, No Compulsion

No matter what the skill being taught, the success of good K-9 training depends completely on the trust between handler and dog. That is why the best training should be done without force or compulsion. Instead, experts say, good training must be based on praising the dog at each step of the process. Officer Jason Linderman of the Reading, Pennsylvania, K-9 unit agrees wholeheartedly. He says: "We reward [the dogs] with praise, and every time they do something right, it's like they won the Super Bowl. We don't just pet them on the head. You're rolling around on the ground with them hugging them and celebrating."[24]

"Disappointed? Not a Bit"

According to K-9 handler Brady Harrison, finding a dangerous gun that has been used in a murder can be just as important as finding the suspect. He recalls:

My dog Sully and I were involved in tracking a bad guy who had just shot a boy, 15 years old. Sully was on the track of the guy— we were in good shape, but either the guy got in a car and left, or we just lost the track. But the good part was that Sully alerted on this gun—a really dangerous machine gun, an AK-47. That was great—I wasn't disappointed at all that we didn't get the guy. The gun was a huge find—not only could the lab get DNA and possibly fingerprints off it, but where Sully found it was 50 yards away from a playground. That could give you nightmares. So was I disappointed? Not a bit—I was proud of Sully.

Brady Harrison, personal interview, St. Paul, MN, February 8, 2009.

Besides being a more humane way to teach, the praise method is also far more effective than scolding or punishing a dog. In addition, says Edina, Minnesota, K-9 officer Kevin Rofidal, a dog that is praised will be a lot more excited about repeating whatever it was that made its handler so happy. Rofidal recalls working with his dog Kodiak for the first time on jumping hurdles, an exercise used to train dogs to go over fences when pursuing a suspect:

The first time he went over a hurdle, it was just a two-by-four—later, of course, we'd build it up, make it more challenging. But the first time he does it, I take him off

K-9 officer Nicole Rasmussen praises her dog, Chase, for a training exercise well done. Experts say that pleasing the handler is the reason that K-9s work so hard.

and we play for about fifteen minutes, then I put him away. And Kodiak thinks to himself, "That was so cool—I got undivided attention for fifteen minutes, just for going over that hurdle." Then he can't wait to do it again.[25]

But even more important, when a handler praises the dog for doing something right—even a small thing—it helps strengthen the bond between them. That bond, which is built on trust and mutual respect, is crucial, since the K 9 and handler must depend on one another as partners. The bond is strengthened even further when, at the end of each training day—and every day after that until the dog is no longer working—the dog goes home with its handler.

A police dog will do the training and perform on the job for several reasons, says Mark Ficcadenti. "There's a number of things that will motivate him," he says. "It might be a favorite toy, or it might be just the thrill of the chase. But ultimately, it's to please the handler. That's why the dog works."[26]

CHAPTER TWO

Cross-Trained K-9s

Dogs that graduate from the police K-9 school are ready to begin working the streets as patrol dogs. However, many police departments around the United States are urging handlers to cross-train their dogs in a more specialized area. Two of the most common choices are narcotics and explosives—two substances police are likely to confront while working on the streets. Not surprisingly, having a partner that can smell the tiniest amount of drugs or just a whiff of the powder in a bullet or an ingredient used to make a bomb could be a huge help to police. And that is exactly what a cross-trained K-9 can do.

The Nose Knows

While human beings depend primarily on sight to interact with the environment, dogs use their sense of smell. The reason is purely physical. There are microscopic cells, called receptors, that gather smells in the noses of animals, including humans. When an animal smells something, that scent is trapped by the receptors, which send the information up into the animal's brain. The brain then helps the animal identify the scent—whether it is food, a predator, or any number of other possibilities.

The big difference between humans and dogs is the number of receptors. While a human has 40 million of them, a dog has nearly 220 million receptors. Depending on the odor, a dog's nose is anywhere between one thousand and ten thousand times more sensitive than a human's nose. Even more remarkable, a dog can smell and catalog between one thousand and ten thousand different smells all at once.

Sergeant Richard Miller, a K-9 handler in Iraq whose dog is trained to sniff out explosives, says it is almost impossible

to imagine how much information a dog can get in a single sniff:

> The best way I can explain it is that if you were to walk into a fast-food place, you'd smell the meat cooking on the grill and the mop bucket they are using to clean up a spill. A dog will smell the fat in the burger charring, the meat cooking, the sesame seeds on the bun, the pickle juice, the type of perfume the cashier is wearing, and a thousand other scents, all at the same time.[27]

Though it seems unbelievable, the nose of this K-9 is thousands of times more sensitive than a human nose. In addition, his brain can catalog thousands of smells at the same time.

Cloning Scent Dogs

In April 2008 the Korean Customs Service announced that they had cloned seven yellow Labrador retriever puppies. The source of the cloning was a highly skilled narcotics dog. Officials explained that it was difficult to find dogs that had the drive, concentration, and patience to screen thousands of airport and harbor travelers and their luggage on a daily basis. The dogs all have the same name—"Toppy," which is a combination of "tomorrow" and "puppy." The cost of each of the seven cloned puppies was between $100,000 and $150,000 in U.S. money. In February 2008 each of them passed a screening behavior test to see if they had the temperament to handle the stress of the job.

"He Would Have Driven Away with All His Dope"

The K-9's ability to identify and catalog even small amounts of scent is extremely valuable to police. For example, in a case when police stop the car of a person suspected of dealing drugs, unless the drugs are in plain view, it might take officers hours to find them. A dog can smell the presence of drugs in seconds and alert its handler immediately.

St. Paul police officer Mike Ernster and K-9 Buzz were called by investigators who had searched a car but found nothing. They had information that the driver was a drug dealer, but searching through the glove compartment and trunk, under the seats, and in other hiding places had yielded nothing. Ernster prepared Buzz for the hunt by asking the dog, "Are you ready to find the drugs? You want to find the drugs?"[28] It was a game to Buzz, and he was immediately ready to play as he climbed inside the car.

It took Buzz no more than two seconds of sniffing to focus in on the center console between the two front seats. And while Ernster directed Buzz to other places—the backseat, the trunk, and the door panels, the K-9 kept coming back to the console, sniffing and scratching at it. Confident in the dog's ability, the officers dismantled the console and found a sock filled with crack cocaine deep inside.

After the discovery Ernster was quick to praise Buzz, noting that the dog's scenting ability was an invaluable tool in getting drugs off the streets. "That ended just because of the dog. Not me, not anybody else, but the dog—using his nose. So

After the K-9 alerted officers to the smell of drugs in this vehicle, officers dismantled the dashboard and found thousands of dollars' worth of cocaine.

without that, the bad guy was going to drive away. He would have driven away with all his dope, and he would have been laughing."[29]

"He Was Like a Five-Year-Old at the Park"

K-9s are cross-trained for scent work in narcotics and explosives in much the same way. They are presented with a range of new scents and are taught that by identifying any of them, they will receive a reward. Not only will their handler praise them and play with them, but they will get a particular toy that is brought out when—and only when—they make a find.

By the Numbers

220 MILLION

Number of scent receptors in a dog's nose

Handlers are instructed to show up on the first day of training with a toy that they know their dog will work hard for. Kevin Rofidal laughs when he recalls going to the pet store with his dog Kodiak, allowing him to choose items that appealed to him. Rofidal says that, much like a young child, Kodiak was interested in many of the toys, not just one. "So I bought a bunch of stuff—a little soccer ball, a little hedgehog—a bunch of things he seemed to really like,"[30] he says.

But though he felt prepared for the first day of narcotics school, Rofidal soon realized that he had hit a snag with Kodiak. As the dogs and their handlers gathered to begin their training, Kodiak no longer was interested in any of his own toys. Rofidal explains:

He kept looking over at this other dog who was being rewarded with this little tugging toy. And Kodiak decided he wanted that one. I mean, I thought we'd brought really cool toys, but Kodiak didn't want any of them. The handler saw what was going on, and was nice enough to lend it to me, and actually ended up letting us keep it. I've

K-9 Harley's reward for working hard in training is getting some time with his favorite toy—a chew made of an old fire hose.

still got it, coming up on seven years now. That's his narcotics toy, what he gets as a reward when he alerts to drugs. It's just a little tug, like I said, nothing special. But he was like a five-year-old at the park looking at what other another kid's got, and wanting it.[31]

"Check, Check, Check"

Once they choose the toy, handlers begin working with their dogs, exposing them to the scents of various substances. For explosives training they become familiar with the scents of ingredients used in making bombs or bullets—among them, gunpowder, black powder, TNT, and nitrates. For drug training, dogs learn the smell of marijuana, cocaine, crack cocaine, methamphetamines, and heroin.

Several methods work in familiarizing the dogs with these new scents, but one that many K-9 trainers use involves five identical wooden boxes. In drug training, for example, when the dog is not looking, the trainer puts a sizable amount of marijuana in one of the boxes. (Marijuana is used because it has a very strong odor and is therefore a good drug to start with.)

The handler then leads the dog to each box and instructs it to "check, check, check." He or she keeps saying the word, so even though the dog does not yet understand what it is supposed to do, the word will gradually become linked to that process. When they get to the box that contains the drugs—called a "hide"—the handler puts the dog into a sitting position. That will be the alert, or signal to the trainer that the dog smells drugs.

A dog sitting when it smells drugs is called a "passive alert." Some dogs that are more high-energy types may alert by scratching or digging at the box. That is called an "aggressive alert." Either way, the moment the dog alerts the handler,

By the Numbers

500

Number of packages a narcotics dog can search in an hour

out comes the new toy. This, explains Rofidal, is when the game gets fun for the dog:

> He's excited, the game is fun now. He's learning the beginning of the process—that when he comes to that odor and he sits, he gets a toy. That's the goal. Anyway, then we take him out of sight for about five seconds, and one of the trainers moves the boxes around so the dog can't predict by the alignment of the boxes which one is the hide. Then we play the game again. We get to the hide, and we make him sit. It goes on, over and over—just repetition. But because there's a toy involved, the dog is having fun.[32]

No Limit

After days of playing the new game with the boxes and the toy, the trainers move the whole game to new places—buildings, offices, city skyways, and outdoors. It is not long, says Rofidal, before there comes a very rewarding moment when all of a sudden, the dog just gets it. "You tell the dog to check," he says, "and he just puts his nose there by the hide, and—you watch—he starts to sit on his own. You don't have to do it for him. He's connected the toy and the drug smell and the sit, so he's figured out what we want from him."[33]

Once the dog has made that connection, training can proceed without using the boxes. At this point, small amounts of drugs can be hidden more secretively in a wider variety of places—behind the headlight of a car, inside a baby stroller, or inside a person's sock. And each time the dog finds the drugs and sits to alert its handler, it is praised and treated to its special toy.

Gradually, the trainer presents more scents for the dog to learn. A dog is officially certified as a narcotics dog when it can identify at minimum the scents of the five most common drugs. However, says Rofidal, trainers often introduce new scents when they have access to other drugs after an arrest of a drug dealer.

An officer relies on his K-9's superior sense of smell in searching for drugs dropped by a fleeing suspect in a city park.

"If we have some opium or ecstasy in custody, we'll train with that, too," he says. "The dogs learn it quickly, so it's not hard for them at all. The dog just catalogs that new scent in his brain. It's really incredible—he can learn a new one today, and a year later—even if he hasn't smelled it since—he'll recall it and sit when he gets a whiff of it."[34]

Getting Around Distracters

In training for narcotics, smelling a variety of drugs and learning to alert a handler is very important. But that alone will not guarantee a K-9's success as a narcotics dog. One of the key things a good narcotics dog must learn is to ignore what are called "distracters"—items associated with drug use or drug dealing but that are not drugs.

Common distracters may be a plastic container used to carry the drugs or a glove used to handle them. Sometimes, too, drugs are cut, or diluted, with substances to make them less potent. Pure cocaine, for example, may be cut with anything from powdered infant formula to talcum powder or cornstarch. These substances are distracters, too.

These scents can be a real problem, for while they might be associated with drug use or drug dealing, they are not narcotics. But they can confuse the dog into thinking that it has found drugs when it really has not. It is important that the dog not alert its handler to those scents when doing a real-life search, says trainer Mark Ficcadenti. "That's why we add distracters when we train the dog," he explains. "We don't want dogs hitting on the smell of a glove or plastic, or someone with talcum powder on their clothes. He has to hit on what's called the signature odor—the scent of the drug itself."[35]

To teach the dogs to alert only to the signature odor, trainers put some of those distracters out when dogs are learning to alert to drugs. And if a dog sits down when it smells one of those distracters, handlers just keep moving the dog along, so it is clear that is not what the handler wants. Eventually, the dog learns that its job is to respond only to the signature odor.

K-9s and Public Relations

More and more police departments are finding that their K-9 teams are an important way to maintain a good relationship with the community. Schools, civic organizations, and community groups are very interested in the work the teams can do. One handler says that he and his fellow K-9 officers give out what look at first like baseball cards, but are actually color photos of each handler and his or her dog. "Kids like them—we get asked all the time if we've got cards. It's a good way for us to stay connected with the people we serve. Without our dogs, we'd just be boring old police officers."

John Buchmeier, personal interview, St. Paul, MN, February 23, 2009.

Coffee Grounds and Liquid Tide

Sometimes the distracters can be intentionally added to a package of drugs by the dealers. Many people who sell drugs try to mask the scent in case they are stopped and searched by a K-9 officer. In fact, they go to incredible lengths to disguise the smell. Andy Stender and his first K-9 partner, Sam, went to a home in Minneapolis to investigate a tip that the owner of the home had a suitcase containing drugs. Stender still remembers how amazed he was when Sam quickly alerted to the package, which was wrapped heavily in plastic with liquid Tide laundry detergent and coffee grounds poured around it to mask the scent.

Sometimes drug dealers try to fool dogs by simply hiding drugs in the most unlikely and hard-to-reach places. Some carry soda cans or hair spray containers with screw-on bottoms, where drugs or other things can be hidden. They may have special compartments for drugs built into the dashboard or even the gas tank of their cars.

Mark Ficcadenti smiles when he acknowledges the lengths drug dealers will go to in order to disguise their merchandise, but he says that usually such efforts are not successful. "I'm very confident in our dogs," he says. "Once they know what odor we need them to respond to through training, they're able to discriminate that through masking agents, chemicals, and other distracters. We know how the drug dealers do it, we know how to train for it, and we are getting really good at using it to our benefit. Our training just gets better and better."[36]

False Positives

Like dogs trained in narcotics detection, bomb dogs face their own challenges. Ironically, the bomb dog's keen sense of smell and recognition of various ingredients of explosives such as gunpowder and nitrates can occasionally lead to mistakes. Called "false positives," these are situations in which the dog alerts to the scent of an explosive ingredient in something harmless.

Nitrates, for example, are present in a number of other products besides explosives, including certain felt-tip markers, tennis balls, shoe polish, and fertilizer. When Officer Brady Harrison was ordered to do a routine bomb sweep before an important political rally in St. Paul in the summer of 2008, his dog Sully alerted immediately to a camera bag left on the ground by a television photographer. "I thought to myself, 'What the heck?'" remembers Harrison. "I went over and asked the guy what was in there, and he just said it was camera batteries. I took a look, and that's all it was. Sully had alerted to a very, very tiny amount of nitrates, that's all."[37]

Harrison had a similar experience when he and Sully did a bomb sweep before a big concert in the Twin Cities. "Sully gave me a sit right next to a big box on the stage," he remembers. "The band's crew had forgotten to tell us that they were planning to do a big pyrotechnics [fireworks] display during the concert." And because fireworks are made with black powder (another ingredient of explosives), Sully had reacted to the scent. "It wasn't Sully's mistake," says Harrison. "He was doing exactly what he was supposed to do. It just happens that these ingredients show up in other places than guns and bombs."[38]

"It's a Lot to Ask of a Dog"

For K-9 teams who work for law enforcement agencies other than police departments, explosive work is mostly screening. For those on Washington State Patrol's Explosive K-9 Unit, for example, there are long, ten-hour working days. Since the attacks of September 11, 2001, Homeland Security has demanded that people using ferries, subways, trains, and airports in the United States be randomly searched to make certain no one is carrying an explosive device.

But the numbers are overwhelming, with 25 million riders using twenty terminals annually in Washington's ferry system alone. Sniffing hundreds of passengers and their luggage is difficult and time-consuming. "It's a lot to ask of a dog," says Rob Richey, one of the unit's trainers. "The dog has to have a lot of stamina. We're asking them to work for hours on end."[39]

Not only are the days long and physically draining, but there is hard work that, because of its nature, can be not only difficult, but boring. "The good news is there aren't many explosives or guns turning up," says one airport K-9 security officer. "The bad news for the dogs is they could tend to get bored. And you want them anything but bored, when they're doing an important job like this."[40]

"The Whole Thing Is a Game"

Bomb dog handlers agree that it is a challenge for these dogs to stay focused on the job without success. "Remember, the whole thing is a game," says Brady Harrison. "The dog's not thinking, 'Oh, I hope I find this explosive device so it doesn't blow up a building and kill a bunch of people.' They're pretty much in the 'I hope I find something so I can get rewarded with my toy' frame of mind. They work because we make it a game."[41]

Keeping the dog sharp, alert, and focused is part of the handler's job. Some law enforcement agencies, such as the Bureau of Alcohol, Tobacco and Firearms (ATF), feed their dogs only when they find a bomb. Since explosive finds are fortunately rare, that means handlers like ATF agent Sheila Fry must create opportunities for her dog Andy to find explosives so that he can eat. Three times each day, Fry hides shell casings or explosive ingredients in buildings, cars, or even open outdoor spaces and lets Andy find them. When he alerts to the scent, she hand-feeds him to remind him that finding explosives means an immediate, tasty meal.

Drug dealers hide their merchandise in places where they think the K-9s will not smell it. Here, cocaine hidden by a car's gas cap was quickly found by the dog.

While city police K-9s do not have that same feeding policy for their dogs, they still must find ways to keep their dogs sharp if real-life gun or other explosive finds are not an everyday occurrence. They, too, create hides containing guns, ammunition, or other explosives so that the dogs have an opportunity to find them.

The more ongoing training that K-9s get in their area of expertise, the more secure their handlers are when working with them. And especially for police K-9s and their handlers, nowhere is that security and trust more important than when they are patrolling the streets, where illegal drugs and gun crime can create dangers around every corner.

CHAPTER THREE

On the Streets

Once their K-9 school and cross-training work is completed, the dogs and their handlers are ready to apply what they have learned to real-life situations. Some police departments, especially in smaller cities and towns, may use their K-9 teams primarily on an on-call basis, such as when a suspect is at large or a car needs to be searched for drugs.

But for the majority of larger cities, K-9 teams work primarily as patrol officers. They respond to domestic assaults, robberies, and even issue traffic tickets—just as do other patrol officers. However, when a high-risk situation arises—an armed robbery, or if a murder suspect is fleeing, for example—the K-9 team is always called.

"It's a Learning Process"

Even with the months of intensive training behind them, however, the dogs are rookies. "They're like brand-new police officers, in a way—totally without real experience," says trainer Mark Ficcadenti. "Each handler, each dog has their own unique personality, and no two are alike. They've got to get used to one another, and that takes time."[42]

Ficcadenti says that it is important to remember that K-9s are not machines and there will always be problems along the way. "That's all this dog business is," he shrugs. "Those problems may start right away, or six months later. If you don't have some little issue with the dog today, you'll have one tomorrow. It's a learning process—you figure out how to correct each one as it comes up."[43]

No one has to convince Officer Brady Harrison of that. The first time he commanded his dog Sully to apprehend a real-life

Although highly trained, a K-9 may still encounter problems with commands as happened during this Iraqi police dog demonstration in 2008.

suspect who would not cooperate, Harrison watched the dog in disbelief. Instead of rushing at the suspect and biting him, Sully just sniffed at the man's leg. "Then," recalls Harrison, "the guy goes, 'I give up.' Amazing. The dog did nothing but sniff the guy's pant leg and wag his tail at me. I called the trainer and said, 'Mark, you didn't give me a police dog!'"[44]

Harrison says that he and the trainer kept working with Sully, allowing him to get used to confronting a suspect and biting him by going back to the training decoy with the bite suit. With patience and work, Sully finally understood what was expected of him out on the streets. Harrison says that was a red-letter day, when he realized Sully was going to be a good partner:

We had a hotel being renovated, and a couple of guys were in the process of walking out with stolen computers and TVs from the site. I see the one guy running from us, and I gave my standard command, "Stop now or I'll send the dog—and you'll get bit." But he didn't stop. So I unhook Sully's lead and told him to get the guy. And Sully took him right down! I round the corner, and there he is, holding the bad guy by the leg. That was the night I knew he had what it takes—and he's consistently gotten better and better since then.[45]

Trust the Dog

As each team develops a working relationship, the partners learn to trust one another. The dog learns to trust that its handler will be consistent with it, both in providing instructions and in giving praise when the dog does the job asked of it. Handlers learn that although they cannot smell what their dog smells, they must trust what the K-9 is telling them.

Sometimes that trust is the only evidence a police officer has in deciding whether or not to conduct a search of someone's vehicle, for example. In July 2007 a sheriff's deputy in the little town of Zebulon, North Carolina, had to decide whether to risk destroying a brand-new set of tires on a suspect's vehicle solely on the basis of what his dog was telling him. The K-9 handler, Deputy Roy Wilbourne, was called when another patrol officer stopped a tour bus after it ran a red light.

Both officers were somewhat suspicious of the tour bus, which has become a common type of vehicle used by drug smugglers since airport security was tightened after the September 11 attacks. When Wilbourne's K-9 partner, thirteen-year-old Thor, did a quick sniff of the outside of the bus, he gave an aggressive alert for narcotics, scratching energetically at

By the Numbers

$22,000

Cost in 2008 for a squad car equipped for a K-9 team

Becoming A K-9 Handler

Job Description:

A K-9 handler is first a police officer, with all of the responsibilities that job entails—protecting the community, catching lawbreakers, maintaining order, and working to prevent crimes from occurring. The K-9 handler is partnered with the dog and is responsible for the training, health, and living conditions of the animal.

Education:

In most police departments in the United States, the K-9 officer must have a college education, followed by formal classroom training in a police academy. After that, the officer is finally assigned a dog, and together they train in patrol work and possibly narcotics or explosives detection.

Qualifications:

All police must be in good physical shape, but it is even more important for the K-9 officer, who must be able to keep up with the dog while tracking lawbreakers. A K-9 officer must like dogs and have a great deal of patience to be consistent and encouraging with the K-9.

Salary:

As of 2008 most departments do not give a salary increase for K-9 work. The standard pay for a police officer varies nationwide, ranging between $49,500 and $65,000 for an officer with three years on the job.

the rear tires. On the basis of Thor's alert, the deputies took the bus into custody, jacked it up, and removed the new tires. After sawing each of them open, they found custom-made steel containers that fit inside each of the tires, behind the rims. In the containers was more than 70 pounds (32kg) of cocaine.

Probable Cause

Police K-9s are so reliable in their detection that U.S. courts consider an alert for drugs or explosives on the outside of the vehicle a good enough reason to allow police a careful search inside the vehicle. Laws protect Americans from being singled out for illegal searches. It is not permitted for police officers to search a person's car randomly unless they have a good reason. Such a reason is called "probable cause."

A suspicious car stopped by police can be searched when a K-9 alerts officers. In this case, drugs were found on board, in the center console.

A K-9 cross-trained to search for explosives can easily smell the gunpowder in a gun such as this one, hidden in ground cover.

Police know that without being able to show probable cause, the person cannot be charged with a crime—even if he or she has a ton of illegal drugs in the car. Other probable causes allowing a search could be if drugs or a gun are in plain view of the officer or if the driver gives permission for a search. According to K-9 officers few drivers refuse the request, perhaps because they believe that the weapons or drugs are so well hidden that they will not be found.

Experienced K-9 teams laugh at that. Says Glenn Olson:

You almost feel sorry for the bad guy who gives you the go-ahead to search his car, when it takes your dog about three seconds to find the gun he's hidden behind the dash, or the eight-ball [an eighth of an ounce, or 3.5g] of crack they've got stashed in an old McDonald's bag under the front seat. And then, after you praise your dog, love him up, and play tug of war or whatever, you don't feel sorry for the guy at all. Just proud of your dog.[46]

The Most Exciting Part of the Job

But while K-9 handlers on patrol do many such searches for drugs and explosives, most say that the most exciting part of their job is when they need to use the dog's amazing sense of smell to locate a human being. Whether it's a homicide suspect huddled in a building or garage hiding from a searching squad car, or a burglar running through the alleys of a city in the middle of the night, the police dog excels at identifying and following human scent.

Unlike the scent of drugs or explosives, this type of scent is well known to dogs, since every person they have encountered has one. When dogs are tracking human scent, however, they are not smelling the things people often smell about each other—aftershave lotion, cigarette smoke on clothing, or garlic from last night's pizza. In fact, they are likely smelling what a human could never detect, which is the scent of dead skin cells, called skin rafts, which the human body sloughs off by the thousands every minute. Experts believe that dogs are capable of locating the scent of those skin rafts and following it until they get to the person who is shedding them.

Following a scent is second nature to dogs. The trick for the handler is communicating to the dog what it is being asked to do with that particular ability. First, the dog needs to learn the word for what it is being asked to do. And like so many other aspects of K-9 work, this starts in training.

Learning to Track

Officer Kevin Rofidal began by taking his dog Kodiak to a park and putting him in a tracking harness, an arrangement of straps around the dog's body that gives a handler more control over the K-9, but without putting as much stress on the dog's neck as a regular collar. The harness quickly becomes a signal to the dog when they are out on patrol that it is expected to look for humans, as opposed to drugs. Rofidal put the dog in a down position, so the dog could watch what his handler was going to do next:

I started walking, laying a track, in a straight line. I didn't walk like I usually do, but instead, I dragged my feet, so I was leaving a lot of scent. Then I turned around after going about 50 feet, and walked back on that same track, so it's got a really strong scent. When I got back to where Kodiak was waiting, I brought him on his lead over to where the track started. I just let him stand there, and all of a sudden the dog starts kind of tasting the air—that's the best way I can describe it. He knew something was there, in front of him. And then as soon as he does that, you say the word "Track."[47]

Once the dog is tasting the air, the handler begins to walk along with the dog on lead, along the track. The handler brushes the ground with his hand to stir up the scent a bit more and keeps repeating the command "track." And when they have followed the entire length of the track, the dog receives lavish praise and a toy—different from the toy that it gets for narcotics or explosives work. "Most important," says Rofidal, "is that he gets about 15 minutes of play time with me, and he likes that a lot."[48]

Over the next days and weeks, the track gets more challenging. The handler changes the length or adds curves to it. Eventually, the handler gets another person to make the track, so the dog understands that the "track" command does not mean only its handler's scent. As they practice more and more, the dog becomes adept at using its nose to find anybody.

The Call

The instant the K-9 team on patrol gets a call that a suspect is on the run—either in a car or on foot—the handler knows time is critical. Many times a suspect

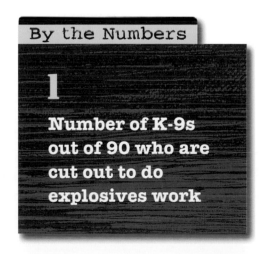

By the Numbers

1

Number of K-9s out of 90 who are cut out to do explosives work

The K-9 Patrol Car

One of the biggest expenses in adding a K-9 to a police department is the addition of a specially equipped squad car. The car itself is much the same as a regular squad car, with a light bar on top and a laptop inside for the officer, who needs to get information about a vehicle or driver quickly. However, since the K-9 team does not transport suspects to jail, the car has a mini-kennel rather than a backseat. The surface of the mini-kennel is easy to keep clean, and there is a spillproof water bucket. In addition, many officers carry a remote device on their belts with which they can pop the K-9's door open. If the officer is hurt or needs help in a hurry from the dog, he or she needs only to press a button and the K-9 is released from the car.

speeding to get away will ditch the vehicle or sometimes even crash it, and then flee on foot. In a case where the suspect is driving, the K-9 officer will speed up to position the squad car directly behind the suspect's vehicle, so that if the suspect ditches the car, the handler and the K-9 will be ready to chase him or her.

Interestingly, K-9s often realize that a tracking opportunity is coming up long before the handler opens the car door and puts the harness on the dog. Many officers say their dogs begin whining and pacing in the back of the car when the handler turns the siren and lights on. Some even swear that their dogs can tell the difference between a medical radio dispatch and a crime that most likely will mean a K-9 is needed to track, just by the level of excitement in the voices of the dispatcher and police on the radio. Once they realize they are going to be working on a chase, the dogs begin to bark and scratch at the center grill separating

An officer helps a K-9 over a fence while tracking a suspect. Many K-9s sense that a tracking opportunity is at hand even before they are released from the squad car.

the car's kennel from the front seat, as though the car cannot get there quickly enough. "If some of these dogs could drive the car, they would," says Mark Ficcadenti. "They'd kick you to the side and drive it themselves."[49]

When the K-9 team arrives on the scene of a ditched or crashed car and the suspect has fled, it is the handler who gives most of the directions to the street officers. The K-9 officer directs the others to set up a perimeter, a set area in which the police will try to contain the suspect. The size of the perimeter depends on a number of factors, such as the weather, or if officers believe the suspect is moving slowly—because of a wound, for example. The size of the perimeter might also take into account whether the suspect has any known friends or family within the area—which may indicate he or she will take refuge with them. While the K-9 team is tracking the suspect, the rest of the officers will position their squad cars around the perimeter with their lights and blinding white spotlights on to help illuminate the area.

"We're really good at perimeters," says K-9 officer John Buchmeier. "I've had bad guys I've just arrested comment on that, like if they've been hiding up on a roof or somewhere where they could see the whole thing unfold. They'll say, 'Boy you guys really set that perimeter up fast.' They're right, we do—we train for it. Perimeters make a huge difference for K-9 teams."[50]

Reading the Tracking Dog

In addition to establishing the perimeter, the handler chooses one or two "cover officers" to come along on the track. The handler's job is to work with the dog as it tracks. The cover officers jog behind and to the sides of the handler and maintain radio communication with the perimeter. When the suspect is located and is either apprehended by the dog or surrenders, it is the cover officers who will search the suspect for weapons and put him or her in handcuffs. The handler's job is to order the dog to release the bite (if the K-9 apprehended the suspect), and then to praise the dog immediately for a job well done.

Once the cover officers arc in place, the handler usually takes the dog to the last place a suspect was known to be—whether it be a ditched car or a store that was just robbed. The dog needs to find the scent that is likely the strongest, since it is the most recent, compared to the scent of other people's skin rafts that have been shed in that same area. K-9 handlers readily admit that there is no ironclad guarantee that when the dog is tracking, it is actually following the suspect. Officer Kevin Rofidal explains:

> Say a convenience store was robbed. For all we know, when we take him to the last known spot where the suspect was seen, he's following the scent of the last guy to come in buying milk. You don't know at first. But as the track goes on, if it's the right guy, you usually get a pretty good idea, because you see things that indicate someone is running away—a track that shows the person is going through backyards, or going over fences, things that indicate the human is in a hurry.[51]

Handlers say that by reading their dogs, they can almost always tell when they are just looking for a scent and when they actually latch on to a human scent. Depending on the individual dog, it may be the way the tail rises or falls, or if the ears go back. Rofidal says:

> Every dog is different, I think, just like people. I think each one might have his own mannerisms. Kodiak's tail drops way down when he's on a human scent, and when he's just looking, his tail is high. It's just getting used to your dog, and observing him. Nothing in the manual, no one told me. But if I don't learn that after hours and hours of watching how he works, I'm not pulling my weight as his partner.[52]

Medallion

The United States Police K-9 Association, Inc.
Region XII

Officer Rofidal and K9 Kodiak
Of The
Edina Police Department

Is Hereby Presented This Citation For Having Directly Aided In The Capture And
Arrest Of A Criminal Who Was Endangering The Lives And Property Of The People Of
The Community. This K-9 Team, While In The Performance Of Their Duties, Reflected
Only The Highest Tradition Of Police Service And The Profession They Represent.
Given The 1st Quarter of 2007

President

Awards Chairman

Secretary

Though K-9 teams do not purposely seek recognition, city governments sometimes award them for their hard work.

How It Ends

Tracking pursuits end in various ways. In most instances, the dog locates the suspect. At that point the officer orders the suspect to surrender, warning that if he or she does not, the suspect will be bitten by the dog. Some suspects ignore the warning and take off running again. In that case, the handler will release the dog, and the K-9 will subdue and hold the suspect until the cover officers can make sure he or she is not armed or otherwise a threat.

When the suspect is put in handcuffs, the cover officers will report that they have apprehended the suspect and call for one of the cars on the perimeter to come and transport him or her to the police station for booking. If the dog has bitten the suspect, it is standard procedure to take the suspect to a hospital emergency room, where doctors can check out any wounds before the suspect is taken to police headquarters.

However, in many cases, when suspects hear the warning that the police dog is about to be released, they give up quickly. Just the threat of an encounter with the K-9 is very often enough to defuse the situation. Nothing exemplifies this more than a situation that developed during a robbery in progress at a Michigan restaurant one night. The officer who answered the call realized the burglar was still in the restaurant and yelled to the man that he was sending a dog in. However, as he radioed for a K-9 unit, he learned all of the K-9 teams were busy. According to K-9 historian Marilyn Jeffers Walton, the officer realized he could not wait. "With his head thrown back and with his most fearsome tone," she reports, "the officer imitated the loud bark of a police dog. The burglar came out with his hands up."[53]

"Tyke Really Knocked Me off My Feet"

No matter how many times they have seen K-9s shine when it comes to the tracking and apprehension of criminals, veteran handlers often say their dogs never cease to surprise them. Head K-9 trainer Mark Ficcadenti has been a St. Paul police officer since 1984 and a K-9 handler since 1990. But he says just when he thinks he has seen all of the abilities that the trained K-9 has, one of the dogs will amaze him by showing perception or intelligence that he has not seen before.

He cites a situation that happened several years back. Late one night he was called to a large downtown department store for a "burglary in progress," meaning that it was likely that the burglar was still on the premises. He and another K-9 trainer were to do a sweep of the store—tracking in a confined area by using their dogs to see if there was any human inside. But as he recalls, he was doubtful they would find anything:

> The store had been having trouble with their burglar alarms all week, so we thought it was more than likely a false alarm. Anyway, we'd been in there almost three hours, and we'd kept hitting alarms as we moved our way up to the top floors. We searched the last area, top floor, without finding anything, and I remember telling my dog—his name was Tyke—"Let's get out of here." But the dog did something I'd never seen him do before. He circled back, all the way to a dressing room on the far end of the building. He was off lead, and did it totally on his own.[54]

Ficcadenti said he was puzzled as to why Tyke would go back to an area that they had cleared already, but he followed the dog. He saw Tyke walk into one of the cubbyholes in the dressing room and jump up toward the ceiling, barking. Ficcadenti says:

> I looked up, shined my flashlight up there, and the second I noticed a ceiling tile a little out of place, the guy jumped out of the ceiling and came down hard down on top of me and the dog. The guy was really big and very strong, and both of us were trapped underneath him. But it ended when Tyke was able to struggle free, and bite the guy's arm to apprehend him. Then I searched him for weapons and handcuffed him. The guy had been hiding in the store since closing time, and had about $30,000 worth of merchandise he was stealing in one of those big mail bins on wheels. But the burglar alarm had tripped, and we'd sort of flushed him up to the top floor—and into the ceiling.[55]

Ficcadenti still shakes his head when he thinks about it. "I've never seen that before. Tyke just decided on his own to go back—he just knew the guy was there, and decided to do it. And not only that—but he had the courage to fight the guy and subdue him without me having to tell him to do it. I'm telling you, Tyke really knocked me off my feet that day."[56]

CHAPTER FOUR

Lives on the Line

K-9 officers are aware that any situation in which they are involved has an element of risk. However, some situations by their very nature are much riskier than others and can put the lives of both dogs and their handlers in danger. An example is when police are tracking a suspect who is armed, who might have just shot someone, and who has no intention of surrendering peacefully to police. In situations like this, K-9 officers know there is a chance they could be the next target.

Mark Ficcadenti says that risk is simply part of the job of a K-9 team and that they prepare for it. "I have no hesitation sending K-9 teams, including myself, into situations where they'd be fired upon, because that's our job," he says. "We train for that daily, we train for that monthly, and we look forward to that opportunity."[57]

In the Kill Zone

One of the ways police officers measure the risk in a particular case is how much they are exposed in what is called the "kill zone." That is the spot that is the most likely place for an officer to be ambushed by an armed suspect. Sometimes it is a large, open space, as in one case on a winter night in 2008. A fifteen-year-old boy had been shot on his front porch by an acquaintance. The shooter, a nineteen-year-old, fled on foot with the gun, and K-9 officer Brady Harrison and his partner Sully were called in to search for him. Harrison remembers:

> Yeah, I was nervous. If the guy's got a gun and has just murdered somebody, we've got to assume it's a possibility that he'll shoot at us. A witness had said the gun

Before pursuing a suspect they believe is armed, two K-9 officers help one another with their SWAT gear.

was an AK-47, which is an automatic—basically a machine gun like the ones you see guys in Afghanistan shooting in the air, you know? And even though my cover officers and I were all wearing SWAT gear—bulletproof vest, helmet, they wouldn't have been much good if the guy had shot at us with that gun. AK-47s are really powerful, and can pierce the body armor we were wearing—go right through. And because we were tracking in the middle of a field for a lot of the time, we had no cover.[58]

City streets contain kill zones, too. K-9 officer John Buchmeier says city tracks often leave police dangerously exposed, not because of open spaces, but because of the number of small hiding places a suspect could use. When Buchmeier was called to chase an armed suspect who had just robbed and killed a man, the scent led him and his dog Andy into a dark alley. And although he trusted that Andy would bark when the suspect was close by, Buchmeier was still aware of the dangers: "I remember thinking, threats were everywhere—it wasn't a good place for us. You look one way, there's a fence and bushes, and another way, there's a porch where a guy could crawl under. There are garages and garbage cans for someone to hide behind —just looking around, you say, each one of those is a reason to have the dog."[59]

Sweat, Fear, and Cover Officers

In such dangerous police operations, handlers rely even more on the cover officers. Many say that if possible, they would choose to use other K-9 handlers as cover officers, just because they understand far better than anyone exactly what to do. The handler serving in that capacity would not use a dog, however, because two dogs working a track would distract one another.

Another aspect of choosing a cover officer in dangerous situations is that the person must not be at all fearful of dogs. If the officer is even slightly afraid, it can result in problems in two ways, say handlers. The first has to do with—surprisingly—sweat. People who are frightened or under a lot of stress put out a different type of sweat than when they are exercising or overly warm. This is called apocrine sweat, and dogs are very sensitive to its odor. In fact, when dogs smell apocrine sweat, they get excited because it usually means they are getting close to the frightened suspect—and thus, to their reward. Says Ficcadenti, "It's like candy to the dog."[60] But if a cover officer is nervous about the dog, he or she would be putting out apocrine sweat, too. That would be confusing to the dog and would cause a problem for the tracking operation.

During a track, a cover officer (left) has his gun drawn to protect the handler and the dog. Once the dog leads them to the suspect, it is the cover officer's job to handcuff the suspect and call for a squad car to pick him or her up.

But there is another drawback to having a fearful cover officer, notes handler Harrison. "I think more about them being distracted," he says. "I don't want guys who are afraid, because I'm thinking, hey, you're not going to be watching my back, because you're going to have your eye on the dog so he doesn't bite you. I need the cover officers to be doing their job. *I'll* watch the dog."[61]

Sending the Dog

Once they discover where a suspect is hiding, K-9 handlers are reminded that these dangerous situations are another reason they have dogs. Often the hiding place is a perfect place for an armed suspect to fire at his or her pursuers—a place that could be too risky for officers to approach. Glenn Olson explains:

> That's what the dogs are for. It's just a fact of life for a K-9, that they go in whenever it's too dangerous to send an officer. I'm not saying you'd send in a dog needlessly to its death—not a suicide mission, of course. But sometimes if it's a choice between sending a human and the dog in a situation like this, you send the dog. They're highly trained and motivated, and can get the job done.[62]

When John Buchmeier tracked a robbery and homicide suspect to a garage in a St. Paul alley, for example, he had no choice other than to send in Andy. It was a dark, confined space, and there was no way of knowing who was inside and what weapons the suspect might be carrying. The dog had alerted to a garage door that was slightly ajar, and after giving his warning to the suspect to surrender, Buchmeier let Andy go in—still on a long, 15-foot (4.6m) leash. Buchmeier says he did not know for certain that the suspect was in there, but within seconds, all doubt was gone. "He just plowed though that door," Buchmeier says, "and the next thing you know, the lead goes tight, like when you're fishing, and I could hear the guy yelling."[63]

"The Dumb End of the Leash"

There is a lot of emphasis on training the K-9 to work successfully in the field, but there are important lessons the handler must learn, too, according to Kevin Rofidal.

> I think one of the most common mistakes I've seen handlers make—including myself—is not knowing when to keep your mouth shut. A lot of times, it's easy to second-guess the dog, maybe think you know more than he does. Like if he's tracking, and is pulling a certain way, you might be tempted to redirect him because the way the dog wants to go isn't the way you think the bad guy would go. It's better just to be quiet and let him work. The reality is, I'm probably the dumb end of the leash.

Kevin Rofidal, personal interview, Edina, MN, January 31, 2009.

When the suspect finally came out and was handcuffed by the cover officers, Buchmeier told Andy to go in again to search for anyone else who could be hiding in the garage. There was no one else, and after double-checking himself, Buchmeier praised his dog for a job well done.

SWAT Operations

The most dangerous situations of all are operations handled by an elite part of the police department known as the Special Weapons and Tactics (SWAT) team. The SWAT team might be used in hostage situations or those in which an armed suspect has barricaded him- or herself in a building or home. Sometimes these situations involve an armed person on the run in a neighborhood, a sniper, or a person who is wanted for an extremely dangerous crime, such as firing on a police officer.

Because grenades and other loud noises during a SWAT mission can hurt a dog's ears, some handlers fit their dogs with special devices to muffle the loudest sounds.

Getting a K-9 Used to Gunfire

1   While the dog is having fun with its handler on the agility course, have an officer fire a starting pistol or some other light gun from 50 yards (46m) away or more.

2   This can be repeated once a day, until the dog does not show any fear.

3   Decrease the distance between the firing gun and the dog by a little bit.

4   Increase the caliber of the rounds, which will make the gun louder.

5   Continue to take "baby steps" with the dog, not proceeding to a shorter distance or a larger caliber round until the dog is ready.

6   Eventually, with patience from the handler, the dog will be able to tolerate the handler firing a gun while next to it.

SWAT teams train for these apprehensions with military precision, and tactics are a huge part of what they do. They are skilled in weapons that are usually outside the realm of regular police work—machine guns, stun grenades, chemicals such as tear gas or pepper spray, and high-powered rifles for snipers. And more and more SWAT teams are adding K-9s to their ranks.

But not every dog—even highly trained police K-9s— can qualify for SWAT work, says Officer Andy Stender, who, in addition to his K-9 work, serves on the Minneapolis Police Department's SWAT team. Stender explains:

It really takes a certain kind of dog—I think the two main things are confidence and focus. The dog has to have both. Sometimes there's seven, eight guys all together with shields and machine guns, and the dog can't care about them at all. He can't get caught up in what they're doing. He can't get distracted by gunfire, gas, and all the other things that can be part of a SWAT operation.[64]

Leapfrog

In many SWAT operations the dog's main job is to locate the suspect. In the case of a suspect who has barricaded him- or herself in a building, for example, the K-9 and handler are in the first line, called the entry team. Often SWAT teams use the element of surprise, so they are very quiet as they assemble at the site. That means the dog needs to be especially quiet. A dog who barks or whines with excitement could alert the suspect inside. For that reason, the K-9 on SWAT duty learns to obey hand signals as well as verbal commands.

On a prearranged signal, the entry team breaches, or breaks down, the door and begins searching for the suspect. Stender says that once the first line is in, he begins feathering out his dog Harley's leash a little at a time. If the dog does not find anyone, the SWAT team advances as far as Harley has checked. The team always verifies what the dog has done, as Stender explains:

> My dog is good, but there's no such thing as a perfect dog. He goes first, and then we follow and check it ourselves. Then I'll feather him out a bit more, and we double check again. It's like a leapfrog technique. When the team moves, we need to be absolutely 100 percent sure that there's nobody behind us, nobody that got missed hiding in a room. That could be disastrous, because he could get us from behind.[65]

Darkness and Noise

Sometimes the location is smaller, in which case different tactics are used. Ficcadenti recalls a SWAT operation in which he and his second dog, Shadow, were involved. The suspect was a sexual predator who had used a shotgun to fire at agents who tried to arrest him. The agents then requested a SWAT team assist them in arresting the suspect.

Refusing to talk face-to-face with police, the suspect had instead written a series of notes and slipped them under the door of his apartment. Ficcadenti says that officers were certain he was setting them up for disaster. "His plan was to get us closer and closer to the door," he explains, "and then use his shotgun to fire through the door at us."[66]

SWAT teams often use distracters in the moments before they breach an entryway, as a means of disorienting and confusing an armed suspect. In this case they had turned the electricity off, so it was very dark. Also, some of the team members launched tear gas through the apartment windows. Others were going to fire four grenades called "flashbangs," which create a blinding white light and make a loud noise. Ficcadenti remembers:

> The plan was that after they sent the fourth, we'd kick in the door. After the third, I sent the dog, and as he ran in, he leaped over the fourth one just as it exploded. The entry was completely dark and smoky from the gas. But I could see Shadow, like he was on a line, running fast right back to the bathroom. Then I see Shadow thrashing his head, back and forth, back and forth, and I said to my guys, "He's got him."[67]

The suspect had buried himself under a huge pile of clothing to protect himself from the tear gas. Shadow had scented him immediately upon bursting through the doorway and had bitten him on the shoulder, holding him until the team could take him into custody.

A Cup of Coffee and a Dog

In some SWAT operations the dog may be used in a trickier way. A SWAT team always includes a negotiator, whose job it is to talk with the suspect to try to get him or her to surrender peacefully. If talks are ongoing it is possible for the handler and dog to move very quietly into a position where the dog could apprehend the suspect.

For example, in a case where a suspect has been barricaded in a building for many hours, the negotiator might offer to send up some coffee and a sandwich as a gesture of goodwill. But instead of placing the paper bag containing the food and coffee where the suspect can easily reach it as he or she opens the door, the negotiator will place it on the hinge side of the door. That means the suspect would have to open the door almost completely to get the bag. As the armed suspect reaches out to get the food, the dog—waiting silently behind the door with its handler—is in a good position to leap at the suspect and apprehend him or her.

A Risk

But the missions all have an element of risk for SWAT teams, and that includes the K-9s that work with them. Officer Andy Stender's first dog, Sam, was severely wounded during a raid on a Minneapolis house. The case involved a mentally ill man who had been given a weekend pass by the facility that was caring for him.

But the man did not return at the end of the weekend, as he was supposed to. In fact, several days went by until the facility asked the Department of Corrections to find him and bring him back. The Department of Corrections knew where the man was staying, and they asked for backup from the SWAT team.

As usual, Stender and Sam were part of the entry team. When Sam was given the signal to run into the house, he quickly found the man in the bathroom. However, the man had a large knife and lashed out at the dog. Bleeding profusely from a deep wound to his neck and shoulder, Sam was rushed to an emergency veterinary clinic. The doctors were able to save the dog, though Stender says it was touch and go. "He actually died on the table," he says. "But the doctors brought him back."[68]

Although Sam's wounds did not kill him, it was soon clear that his days as a police K-9 were over. His windpipe and been severely damaged, so that it could open only halfway—cutting down on the amount of air he could breathe. He would not be able to exert himself as he once had. After receiving a medal of honor from the mayor of Minneapolis, Sam retired from the department, living out the rest of his life with Stender and his family.

"He's One of the Brothers and Sisters of the Department"

All K-9 officers realize the incredible risks their dogs take for them and how crucial the dogs become in their lives. Not only is the dog a partner on the job, but because it lives with the officer, the dog is an important part of the family. St. Paul officer Mike Ernster's first dog, Bert, died suddenly four years ago after doctors found a lump on the dog's spleen during a routine physical.

"I am still as of this last weekend having talks with my daughter about Bert," Ernster says, "and how much she misses him. And this is a girl who was two years old when he passed away. So her memories of him are fresh. Hardly a week goes by where we don't talk about him."[69]

"I don't want anything to happen to him," says Brady Harrison of his dog Sully. "He's a part of my family, he's a part of our K-9 unit, he's part of our department, and he's one of the brothers and sisters of the department. If he does take a round for me, I'm indebted to him for life."[70]

The St. Paul K-9 Unit maintains a cemetery to honor the dogs that have served on K-9 teams. Each grave has a marker, and a life-size statue of a police dog stands guard.

"Let's Go to Work, Rook"

John Buchmeier says it is a sobering fact of life that police dogs' careers are quite short, even if they avoid serious injury on the job. He says:

You figure they don't usually begin working until they're between two and three years old. And they hit their prime at about five or six—they're at the top of their game, you can see it. They're smart, they're fast, they can do it all. But a couple years or so after that, their bodies start to go, even though their noses are still good.

They just slow down. And that can be devastating for them, for these dogs love to work.[71]

Buchmeier's first dog, Ike, developed a problem with his digestive tract. The vet told Buchmeier that the dog could no longer work and offered to put Ike to sleep—an idea Buchmeier rejected. So Ike lives with Buchmeier and his family, as does Buchmeier's new dog, Andy. "It isn't easy," he smiles. "Ike's digestive system is really slow, and not to go into the details—let's just say it involves a lot of medicine and rubber gloves. But he's been a faithful partner for me. How do you say, 'I'll put you down because you've become inconvenient'?"[72]

Officer Mike Davis knows all too well how hard it can be for a dog when it can no longer work. His first dog, Rookie, retired in 2006 and lived with Davis and his family for the last two years of his life—but did not like the fact that Davis would go off to work without him. But as the months went by, Rookie's illness worsened, and Davis knew the most humane thing was to put Rookie down.

> **By the Numbers**
>
> # 40,000
>
> **Number of skin rafts shed by a person per minute**

But he wanted to give his dog an opportunity to feel that he was on the job one last time. The veterinarian was kind enough to come to the house and give Rookie a shot to relax him, so he felt no pain. "We got him prepped, I got my uniform, went back, opened the car door up and said, 'Let's go to work, Rook,'" remembers Davis. "Got him in the back of the car and put him down. One of the hardest things I've ever had to do."[73]

Davis smiles sadly at his new dog, Auggie. "I'm sure that in due time this guy will take the place of [Rook]," he says, "but I still miss him dearly."[74]

CHAPTER FIVE

Rescue and Retrieval, Living or Dead

Another specialty of K-9 work is known as search and rescue, or SAR. Instead of tracking down criminals, however, these dogs are used to locate people after a hurricane or other natural disaster. If a skier disappears when caught in an avalanche, for example, SAR dogs are deployed. The dogs are also valuable in finding someone who is believed to have wandered away from home. In many cases, SAR dogs help find young children who have disappeared or elderly people suffering from Alzheimer's disease who have become confused about their surroundings.

Many SAR handlers are part of sheriff's departments or state patrols. Some work for the Federal Emergency Management Agency, whose job it is to respond when hurricanes, earthquakes, or other disasters strike. But more and more SAR dog handlers are actually private citizens who volunteer their services to help when there is a need.

Intense Training

To become officially certified to do SAR work, dogs and their handlers must go through an intense training period. Colorado SAR trainer Estelle Purvis says that one must really be serious about SAR work, because it is not an activity that can be taken lightly. "It's a huge commitment," she says, "It takes 18 months to two years, and about 500 hours annually for first-time dog handlers and the dogs to become certified."[75]

The reason for the long training time is the physically demanding nature of SAR work. Some of the skills needed parallel those of patrol K-9s. For example, dogs must learn how to track a person's scent and to obey their handlers' commands so that they can work off lead when necessary. They also go through a great deal of agility work. But the level of agility and stamina needed in SAR work is often far beyond what is needed for patrol K-9s.

SAR dogs need to be able to crawl through tight, dark spaces and walk on a narrow plank high in the air without becoming frightened. They must also practice balancing on teeter-totters and swinging bridges so that they are able to keep their footing while searching a shifting pile of rubble in the aftermath of an earthquake or tornado. A dog must be comfortable enough with being handled so that it can ride without fear on a ski lift to find an avalanche victim, be hoisted down into a gully by a hook attached to its vest to find a missing hiker, or be loaded into a helicopter to do a mountain search.

And just as with training a police K-9, these skills are taught as a game, and the dog always gets a reward as he or she learns.

Search and rescue dogs, unlike police K-9s, come in many different breeds, including mixed breeds. Sometimes puppies as young as this one may show signs of the curiosity and scenting ability necessary for the job.

Traveling Scent

The human half of the SAR team has things to learn, too. One of the most important is the movement of scent as it is transmitted through the air. A handler needs to get the dog to the best possible place to scent the missing person. A person's scent, which the dog tracks by following the smell of the skin rafts, is carried by wind currents. The best position to scent, of course, would be that in which the wind blows the scent directly into the dog's face. But to find that position, the dog needs to zigzag, moving back and forth in the search area with the wind from the side, to catch a hint of the scent.

It is also important for handlers to know that the presence of scent can be some distance from the missing person. Scent

The most important skill a search and rescue dog can learn is the ability to track the scent of a missing person.

can pool, or collect in a low spot, when it hits a barrier such as a wall or a group of rocks. Washington SAR handler Mindy Lewis says:

> You can have your dog alerting at the bottom of a bunch of trees, or down in a coulee [a small valley]. And you learn pretty quick that it doesn't mean that's where the [missing person] is located. It's maybe just hit a barrier. A lot of time the person could be high above you, and the scent is drifting down around where the dog is. It helps to know about scent, and how it moves, because you can save a lot of time and energy.[76]

"You Are Just Grateful You're There"

A great amount of an SAR K-9 team's training focuses on building up physical stamina, too. Unlike patrol K-9 teams, for whom two hours on a track is considered unusually long, SAR teams frequently search for days for a missing person in the most challenging terrain. This requires that handlers and dogs are in great physical shape and that they are willing to train two or three times per week, even after they are certified.

Lewis says the work is often grueling. The teams work in all types of weather—heat, snow, and rain. They also work long hours, as Lewis explains:

> The dogs get to the point where they can work at least an hour—usually more, and then they get a 30-minute break. It involves lots of climbing—we're usually nowhere near a trail. Depending on where you're working, it's in ravines, on rocks, on the sides of mountains. For the dogs, the reason they work is the reward. My dog Carson loves this orange and green tennis ball—that's what he gets when he makes a find. I put it in my pocket every time we are doing a search. It's hard to explain how excited he gets when he sees it—he just shivers! For us, we know it's

often a matter of life and death to find the victim in time, but for Carson, it's all a game.[77]

But even with all of the physical challenges and the grueling regimen of training, she says, a find is well worth it. "It's the most exhilarating feeling in the world. You forget how tired you are from getting just a few naps, and how cold you've been for the past two days," she says. "You are just grateful you're there, seeing the relief on the face of the person who thought she was going to die out there alone—when she realizes she's been found."[78]

Looking for a Boy Scout

In March 2007 SAR handler Misha Marshall and her dog Gandalf (named for the wizard in *The Lord of the Rings*) experienced that feeling for the first time. They had trained for a year for SAR work, but this was to be their first real mission. They were part of an SAR job in the Blue Ridge Mountains of North Carolina, searching for a missing Boy Scout. Twelve-year-old Michael Auberry had vanished from his troop's campsite and had not returned, and people were frantic. A state patrol helicopter with infrared scopes had searched the area, but the thick ground cover and many trees made visual tracking impossible.

Even the dozens of volunteers on the ground who had been searching the area were having trouble. The terrain was so thick and dense that humans alone could not penetrate it, as writer Christopher Davis describes:

> Doughton Park [the site of the camp] is located in a bowl on the side of a mountain. It's traversed by heavily vegetated, treacherously steep ridges rising 2,400 feet. Rock overhangs look down into caverns snarled with wild

By the Numbers

20-30

Number of times SAR dogs are called out annually

rhododendron thickets and deadfall. Slippery moss and waterfall spray threaten footing, and thundering streams could drown out a child's cry for help.[79]

Studying regional maps, the SAR teams saw that they needed to search a 30-mile (48km) section of the mountainous area. Although almost 550 human volunteers had been searching, everyone understood that the dogs would be able to accomplish more, in a shorter amount of time. And because the boy had been missing for a number of days, time was critical —especially because the weather was getting colder.

Search and rescue dogs are often able to track missing people after first picking up their scent from a piece of clothing, such as a T-shirt or jacket.

Success—and Gloating

Marshall and Gandalf and the rest of their team met up with another SAR group that had been searching all night. Members of this group were discouraged, for their dogs had not picked up a single scent. However, they did have an item that they shared—an unwashed T-shirt from the boy's backpack that he had left at the camp. They cut it up in little squares so that each handler could let his or her dog sniff it during the track. By becoming familiar with the boy's scent, the dogs would be able to discriminate between it and any other human scent they encountered along the track.

As the team had practiced, they divided the area into assigned territories. Marshall and Gandalf were with two rescuers without dogs and were going to search the steepest area in the grid. They decided that they would climb to the topmost section of their area, and then let the dog zigzag on the way down as he searched for the scent. As they neared the top of a climb of more than a mile, the wind was blowing directly at the dog, who was ranging about 30 yards (27m) ahead of them. Suddenly, Marshall saw Gandalf's head jerk as though he had caught the scent.

Everything sped up at that point. Gandalf ran out of Marshall's sight, behind the steep, exposed face of the cliff. As she hurried to follow him, she saw a young boy—Michael—on the ledge. Marshall and one of the other searchers called to him, telling him that they had come to bring him home safely. As Michael hugged the dog, the SAR team used their radio to alert the others that the boy had been found. Though dehydrated and suffering from frostbite, Michael would be fine.

Over the next few minutes, Marshall watched as Gandalf began exhibiting a behavior SAR handlers call "gloating"—wanting to stay close to his find, as though he were anxious to celebrate. It was, notes Davis, who reported on the rescue, "the equivalent of an NFL receiver dancing in the end zone."[80]

Another Kind of Find

There is another kind of search for which certain dogs train that is related to SAR work. But while SAR dogs are trained primarily for finding living people, cadaver dogs specialize in the scents of a human body that is dead. Experts say that the work

"I Have to Keep My Head"

Though K-9 work can be very rewarding at times, it is a fact that success sometimes means finding a dead body. That, says K-9 cadaver specialist Paul Bryant, can be very stressful for the handler in a way that other types of K-9 work are not:

> You've got to keep balanced. I look at what the dog and I do as closure for someone, so they can say goodbye to a loved one. But on the other hand, when I am in the process of doing a search, I've got to distance myself from what I'm doing. That sounds kind of contradictory, I know. But I can't think of whatever body I'm looking for as a person. I can't. I have to think of the body as evidence. I have to keep my head. Cadaver work is very difficult, and not everyone is cut out for this. I mean, just imagine, you're on a search, you've often got the deceased's family right there beside you, begging you to find their child, their father, whatever. The stress from wanting to do that for someone—and not knowing how the search will turn out—is unbelievable.

Paul Bryant, telephone interview, March 10, 2009.

of a cadaver dog is more difficult than that of other K-9 specialties, simply because of the changing nature of a dead body.

In the first fifteen minutes after death, for example, the body stops producing certain chemicals that protect the lining of the stomach and other organs. The lack of these chemicals allows bacteria to invade these organs, and that results a faint smell detectable by dogs. As the gas from the bacteria increases, it creates a more powerful smell—that of decaying flesh, which humans can definitely smell, too. But there are other stages of decomposition that produce odors that are not nearly as strong. As the body continues to break down, the scent changes, eventually becoming so faint that humans cannot detect it at all.

Training the cadaver K-9 to alert to a dead body is not much different from training a dog to alert to narcotics or explosives. Cadaver dogs are rewarded with praise and a toy when they alert to the smell of a dead human. A handler trains the dogs to ignore the smell of a dead animal, just as a narcotics K-9 handler trains a dog to ignore a distracter such as powdered milk used to dilute a drug. The scent of death can come from any part of the body, too—whether bone, blood, teeth, or tissue.

Some trainers get bones or tissue from medical research laboratories. They wrap small amounts in a piece of cloth for the dog to find. Others collect what they call "dirty dirt"—the

Austrian rescue workers and their dog search for victims of an earthquake in Bam, Iran, in 2003. Experts say that the work of cadaver dogs is more difficult than that of other K-9 specialties.

soil under a dead body that has collected some of the fluids as the body has decomposed. However, in some states, it is illegal to possess human remains—even for training purposes. More and more, however, cadaver trainers use a human-made concoction of chemicals that smells remarkably like the real thing, with names like Pseudo-Corpse or Pseudo-Drowned Victim, which trainers can order online.

An Alert After a Thousand Years

Because the dog can detect even the faintest scent, the remains can be very fresh or many years old. One of the most remarkable finds by a cadaver dog was that of a black Labrador retriever named Alley. She was well known among SAR and cadaver handlers for being exceptionally skilled at finding scents that other dogs could not.

In 2004 her handler, Heather Roche, brought her to Mississippi, where archaeologists had been excavating what was a prehistoric Indian burial ground. Ground-penetrating radar and other technological tools indicated there were bodies nearby, but the archaeologists hoped a cadaver dog could confirm it.

Alley not only alerted to the places where the radar had indicated bodies, she also alerted on another area that no one had looked at. That puzzled the scientists, and because they lacked funding to do more digging, they were not able to investigate it at that time. Two years later, however, they had the funds to do a dig in that area, and they unearthed the remains of a small child—buried at least a thousand years before.

From Missing to Crime Victim

Another important reason to find a body is to learn the circumstances of the disappearance, especially whether or not the missing person has been the victim of a crime. Once a body has been found, medical examiners can determine if the death was an accident, a suicide, or a murder.

A cadaver dog searches a construction site. K-9s are often enlisted to help police determine whether a missing person is a victim of murder, an accident, or kidnapping.

That was the reason handler Paul Bryant of the Philadelphia Police Department was called to the scene of a house in South Philadelphia in August 2001. A woman named Kimberly Szumski had disappeared in May of that year. Her husband, Tom, insisted to authorities that he had no idea where she had gone. Police were stymied, for she had not taken her car, and her credit cards had not been used—giving investigators few trails to follow. And people who knew her insisted that Kimberly would never have gone off and left her two young children. Some were convinced that her husband had killed her, for he had threatened her in the past. But without a body there was no evidence of a crime.

Bryant says that soon after the woman disappeared, he and his cadaver dog Azeem did some initial searches. "We'd searched the Szumski home, and outside, near the home," he remembers. "And because the husband worked as a contractor, we searched a dump site where bulk amounts of those materials are discarded—wallboard, stuff like that. But we found nothing in those searches."[81]

But in August, three months after the disappearance, police got a tip from one of Tom Szumski's workers in his contracting business. The source gave police the addresses of a few sites where Szumski himself had worked during the month of May without additional help. The time period of one of these jobs matched the date when Kimberly Szumski had disappeared. Immediately, investigators sent for Bryant and Azeem.

When they arrived at this site, the K-9 immediately alerted to a basement wall. After breaking the wall down, police found Kimberly Szumski's body wrapped in a plastic sheet and duct tape. A medical examiner later determined that she had been strangled, and her husband (who had committed suicide during the investigation) was believed to have been her killer.

None of this would have been possible without the cadaver dog's alert, although Bryant says it was actually an easy task for his dog. Though the plastic-wrapped body had been placed in concrete, cinder block, and other construction materials before being sealed within the wall, it took almost no time for Azeem to locate it—though humans could not have detected it. "It was like a training exercise for the dog," Bryant says. "It was really fast—thirty seconds, tops. Sometimes, that's just how it happens."[82]

"They Are Still Somebody's Children"

Cadaver dogs are used for another reason, too. Finding the body of a person who has gone missing provides a sense of closure for the family. Even if the missing person is presumed dead, it helps families to have an answer and a body that they can bury. The case of eighty-two-year-old Colin Hale is a good example. Hale, who suffered from Alzheimer's disease, walked away from his assisted living residence in Sandestin, Florida, in July 2008. Though the sheriff's department circulated photos of Hale and asked for the public's help, no one had seen a trace of him.

Eventually, a cadaver search team was called in, and they found what are believed to be Hale's remains. Vision, a three-year-old cadaver dog, alerted on some remains deep in a thorny, overgrown thicket, far beyond what humans could have seen or smelled from the trail, said Nancy Locke, a member of the K-9 team. "They had to crawl to him," she says. "Four wheelers would never have found him."[83]

Locke feels that too often, people—especially elderly people—go missing and are forgotten. She believes that search teams like hers are a good way to approach the problem. Using trained dogs, searchers might have found Hale before he died. "There are so many people out there who deserve to be found," she insists. "I don't care if they are 80-something. They are still somebody's children and we want to bring them home."[84]

The Pile

At no other time in U.S. history have so many K-9 teams—both SAR and cadaver—worked a site than in the aftermath of the September 11, 2001, terrorist attacks. Within minutes of the fall of the towers of the World Trade Center, handlers and their dogs from all over the United States were preparing to travel to New York to help in the SAR mission.

No one was prepared for the sight that awaited them. "The pile," as it became known to rescue workers, was a seven-story mountain of wreckage made up of jagged metal beams, broken concrete slabs, burst heating pipes, and a thick layer of foul-smelling dust. Broken glass lay 8 or 9 inches (20 or 23cm) deep in some areas, and there were deep "black holes"—voids where

"Now I've Seen Everything"

Many of the firefighters helping search in the World Trade Center ruins had never seen SAR or cadaver dogs work. In Nona Kilgore Bauer's book, *Dog Heroes of September 11th*, a Massachusetts K-9 handler named Mark Dawson recalls how surprised the firefighters were at his dog Elvis's ability to move around the wreckage:

> On one mission we were asked to go with a FDNY [Fire Department of New York] truck company into a large space where the only way down into the void was on a ladder. The captain asked whether I wanted his guys to carry my dog down the ladder or if I would do that by myself. I told him Elvis would climb down by himself. We put the ladder at a 45-degree angle. I went down first and then commanded Elvis to come down. Elvis got on the ladder and climbed down. The fire captain looked down at both of us and said, "Now I've seen everything. You guys can do whatever you want."

Quoted in Nona Kilgore Bauer, Dog Heroes of September 11th: A Tribute to America's Search and Rescue Dogs. Allenhurst, NJ: Kennel Club, 2006, p. 53.

a person would plummet 70 or 80 feet (21 or 24m) down if he or she stepped in one. One handler recalled later that he believed he and his dog were on the ground, when actually they were standing on the wreckage of a large fire truck buried in the debris.

Though it seemed highly doubtful that anyone could have survived, searchers were hopeful—especially the New York firefighters who had lost so many of their own in the towers' collapse. Texas K-9 handler Denise Corliss remembers wanting so badly to be able to give them good news, although it seemed impossible for anyone to have lived through the collapse: "The pressure was so great to find survivors, with everyone watching you, especially the firefighters who were hoping you would find one of their brothers. When [my dog and I] walked up to the pile there would be a sea of firefighters like the parting of the Red Sea, watching you go to work, hoping you would find someone."[85]

Grueling Work

It did not take very long for the workers to realize that this was not going to be a rescue mission, but rather one to recover the remains of the victims. Though they worked hard, balancing on the shaking, unstable pile of debris as they sniffed for any scent of a person, those dogs that were trained only for live finds were unsuccessful. One dog emerged from the debris with a torn, scorched teddy bear in her mouth. Her trainer explained that that his dog was unaccustomed to going so long without a find.

> **By the Numbers**
>
> # 250
>
> **Estimated number of K-9 teams working at Ground Zero in September 2001**

The work was long—usually shifts between ten and twelve hours long. Though the handlers and other human workers wore protective gear, the dogs usually worked without any protection. Because of the fires burning deep within the rubble, there were parts of the pile that were extremely hot. However, boots would have been more dangerous than the heat, for they would have made balance and traction on the pile that much more difficult. Veterinarians at the site said that the most common condition for which they treated the K-9s was burned or cut paw pads. But even with such injuries, the dogs were almost always eager to get back to work.

Interestingly, one of the dogs' most valuable functions at Ground Zero had nothing to do with their scenting ability.

Search and rescue dog Gus and his handler search for survivors following the 9/11 terrorists attacks. This was a grueling job for both dogs and handlers, but they kept at it, hoping to find survivors of the tragedy.

With their calmness and friendly ways, the dogs became a welcome distraction for the firefighters and other rescue workers. And in a place where there was so much death, that relief was necessary. Kelly Gordon, a K-9 handler from California, says that just the physical presence of her dog Buddy allowed gruff men who rarely showed their emotions to vent a little. "One firefighter came up to Buddy and put his arms around him and just started crying,"[86] she remembers.

Better and Better

From their high-profile work at Ground Zero, to their search work in the wilderness of Wyoming, to the streets of urban America—the value of K-9 teams is indisputable. More and more law enforcement agencies and police departments are realizing how much the trained dogs and handlers can accomplish.

Of course, those who put their lives on the line each day with their dogs need no convincing how important the work is. "I can't imagine not doing this," Officer John Buchmeier says about his K-9 work for the St. Paul police. "There are so many people who want to do K-9, but there aren't many who get the opportunity. To me, it's the best job in the world. Working with a great partner, helping keep the community safer. That's why I'm lucky, and I know it."[87]

Notes

Introduction: "It's Absolutely Unbelievable"

1. Quoted in *Canine Courier*, "Patrol Catch of the Quarter: SD Cathy Orde and K9 Moose," March 2008, p. 34.
2. Quoted in *Canine Courier*, "Patrol Catch of the Quarter," p. 34.
3. Quoted in Animal Planet, *K-9 Cops: Gangs*, January 28, 2009.
4. Brady Harrison, personal interview, St. Paul, MN, February 8, 2009.

Chapter One: The K-9 Team

5. Glenn Olson, telephone interview, February 1, 2009.
6. Olson interview, February 1, 2009.
7. Mark Ficcadenti, personal interview, St. Paul, MN, February 2, 2009.
8. Andy Stender, personal interview, Minneapolis, MN, January 26, 2009.
9. Quoted in North American Police Work Dog Association, "Choosing Handlers and K-9s." www.napwda.com/tips/index.phtml?id=42.
10. Olson interview, February 1, 2009.
11. Quoted in Mike Perlstein, "Beasts with a Badge," *New Orleans*, November 2008, p. 68.
12. Andy Stender, personal interview, Minneapolis, MN, February 5, 2009.
13. Stender interview, February 5, 2009.
14. Stender interview, February 5, 2009.
15. Stender interview, February 5, 2009.
16. Harrison interview, February 8, 2009.
17. Ficcadenti interview, February 2, 2009.
18. Ficcadenti interview, February 2, 2009.
19. Mark Ficcadenti, personal interview, St. Paul, MN, February 27, 2009.
20. Quoted in Animal Planet, *K-9 Cops: Teamwork*, January 30, 2009.
21. Ficcadenti interview, February 27, 2009.
22. Harrison Forbes, *Dog Talk: Lessons Learned from a Life with Dogs*. New York: St. Martin's, 2008, p. 174.
23. Ficcadenti interview, February 2, 2009.
24. Quoted in Jason A. Kahl, "Training Reveals Police Dogs' Strengths," *Reading (PA) Eagle*, November 13, 2008, p. A2.
25. Kevin Rofidal, personal interview, Edina, MN, January 31, 2009.
26. Quoted in Animal Planet, *K-9 Cops: Teamwork*.

Chapter Two: Cross-Trained K-9s

27. Quoted in Ben Hutto, "Sniffing Out Explosives," *Soldiers*, May 2008, p. 30.
28. Quoted in Animal Planet, *K-9 Cops: Teamwork*.
29. Quoted in Animal Planet, *K-9 Cops: Teamwork*.
30. Rofidal interview, January 31, 2009.
31. Rofidal interview, January 31, 2009.
32. Rofidal interview, January 31, 2009.
33. Rofidal interview, January 31, 2009.
34. Rofidal interview, January 31, 2009.

35. Ficcadenti interview, February 27, 2009.
36. Ficcadenti interview, February 27, 2009.
37. Brady Harrison, personal interview, St. Paul, MN, February 21, 2009.
38. Harrison interview, February 21, 2009.
39. Quoted in Phuong Cat Le, "If the Dog Sits, There's a Bomb," *Seattle Post-Intelligencer Online*, March 10, 2006. http://seatllepi.nwsource.com/local/2624 93_bombdogs10.html.
40. Interview with airport K-9 security officer, Bloomington, MN, February 2, 2009.
41. Harrison interview, February 21, 2009.

Chapter Three: On the Streets
42. Ficcadenti interview, February 2, 2009.
43. Ficcadenti interview, February 2, 2009.
44. Harrison interview, February 21, 2009.
45. Harrison, quoted in Animal Planet, *K-9 Cops: Gangs*, January 28, 2009.
46. Olson interview, February 1, 2009.
47. Rofidal interview, January 31, 2009.
48. Rofidal interview, January 31, 2009.
49. Quoted in Animal Planet, *K-9 Cops: Meet the Elite*, February 13, 2009.
50. John Buchmeier, personal interview, St. Paul, MN, February 23, 2009.
51. Rofidal interview, January 31, 2009.
52. Rofidal interview, January 31, 2009.
53. Marilyn Jeffers Walton, *Badge on My Collar: A Chronicle of Courageous Canines*. Bloomington, IN: AuthorHouse, 2007, p. xix.
54. Ficcadenti interview, February 27, 2009.
55. Ficcadenti interview, February 27, 2009.
56. Ficcadenti interview, February 27, 2009.

Chapter Four: Lives on the Line
57. Quoted in Animal Planet, *K-9 Cops: Violent Crime*, February 4, 2009.

58. Harrison interview, February 8, 2009.
59. Buchmeier interview, February 23, 2009.
60. Ficcadenti interview, February 2, 2009.
61. Harrison interview, February 8, 2009.
62. Olson interview, February 1, 2009.
63. Buchmeier interview, February 23, 2009.
64. Stender interview, February 5, 2009.
65. Stender interview, February 5, 2009.
66. Ficcadenti interview, February 27, 2009.
67. Ficcadenti interview, February 27, 2009.
68. Stender interview, February 5, 2009.
69. Quoted in Animal Planet, *K-9 Cops: Hide and Seek*.
70. Quoted in Animal Planet, *K-9 Cops: Hide and Seek*.
71. Buchmeier interview, February 23, 2009.
72. Buchmeier interview, February 23, 2009.
73. Quoted in Animal Planet, *K-9 Cops: Hide and Seek*.
74. Quoted in Animal Planet, *K-9 Cops: Hide and Seek*.

Chapter Five: Rescue and Retrieval, Living or Dead
75. Quoted in Miles Blumhardt, "Keen K-9s: A Look at the Life of a Search Dog," The Coloradoan. www.coloradoan.com/apps/pbcs.dll/article?AID=/20090301/ENTERTAINMENT06/90301005.
76. Mindy Lewis, telephone interview, March 1, 2009.
77. Lewis interview, March 1, 2009.
78. Lewis interview, March 1, 2009.
79. Christopher W. Davis, "Gandalf and the Search for the Lost Boy," *Reader's Digest*, December 7, 2007, p. 96.
80. Davis, "Gandalf and the Search for the Lost Boy," p. 97.
81. Paul Bryant, telephone interview, March 10, 2009.

82. Bryant interview, March 10, 2009.

83. Quoted in Robbyn Brooks, "Private K-9 Team Recovers Body," *Northwest Florida Daily News,* January 30, 2009, p. A1.

84. Quoted in Brooks, "Private K-9 Team Recovers Body," p. A1.

85. Quoted in Nona Kilgore Bauer, *Dog Heroes of September 11th: A Tribute to America's Search and Rescue Dogs.* Allenhurst, NJ: Kennel Club, 2006, p. 37.

86. Quoted in Bauer, *Dog Heroes of September 11th,* p. 39.

87. Buchmeier interview, February 23, 2009.

Glossary

alert: A signal from the dog to its handler that the dog has detected a particular scent. The signal is often sitting or lying down next to the place where the scent was detected.

apocrine sweat: A type of sweat that a person puts out when he or she is frightened or under severe stress.

bite sleeve: A reinforced arm used by a decoy during apprehension training.

cadaver: Another word for a dead body.

coulee: A small valley.

distracter: A substance that is associated with a narcotic or explosive, but is not actually a narcotic or explosive. Distracters can sometimes confuse a detection dog.

kill zone: A spot that is a likely place in which an officer could be harmed by a suspect during a police procedure.

lead: Another word for a leather leash.

masking agent: A substance added by drug dealers to try to disguise the smell of drugs so that the K-9 cannot detect them.

narcotics: Drugs.

nitrates: Substances that are used to make bombs and other explosive devices.

perimeter: A boundary set up by police, enclosing the area where a suspect is believed to be hiding.

receptor: Tiny cells in the noses of dogs that help them gather and catalog things they smell.

signature odor: The scent of a substance without distracters or masking agents.

For More Information

Books

American Rescue Dog Association, *Search and Rescue Dogs: Training the K-9 Hero.* New York: Wiley, 2002. This is a detailed but highly readable book on training a dog in obedience, agility, and other necessities for the SAR dog. A good chapter on cross-training for cadaver work.

Nora Kilgore Bauer, *Dog Heroes of September 11th: A Tribute to America's Search and Rescue Dogs.* Allenhurst, NJ: Kennel Club, 2006. An excellent book, with beautiful color photographs of the handlers and their dogs.

Marilyn Jeffers Walton, *Badge on My Collar: A Chronicle of Courageous Canines.* Bloomington, IN: AuthorHouse, 2007. Very readable, with stories about police K-9s, search and rescue dogs, and cadaver dogs.

Periodicals

China Daily, "China Starts First Drug-Sniffing Dog Patrol on Flights," January 14, 2009. www.chinadaily.com.cn/china/2009-01/14/content_7397064.htm.

Cassandra A. Fortin, "Putting Partners Through Paces," *Baltimore Sun,* November 2, 2008.

Internet Source

Julia Layton, "How Search and Rescue Dogs Work," How Stuff Works. http://animals.howstuffworks.com/animal-facts/sar-dog.htm.

Web Sites

K-9 Cops, **Animal Planet** (http://animal.discovery.com/tv/k9-cops). This site gives readers and viewers of the popular TV show *K-9 Cops* an up-close look at the work of each handler and his or her dog.

National Association for Search and Rescue (www.nasar.org/nasar/specialty_fields.php). This site contains the most complete information for search and rescue specialists. It offers a special section on training dogs and choosing an SAR dog, and contains interesting articles about finds that dogs have made in recent months.

National Narcotic Detector Dog Association (www.nndda.org). This site gives information about excellence in the field of K-9 detection, with stories about amazing finds by dogs—both in police work and in Iraq by military dogs.

United States Police Canine Association (www.uspcak9.com). This organization is responsible for testing and recertifying police K-9s and their handlers each year. The Web site explains the certification process and highlights some of the most up-to-date ways that police are training their dogs in narcotics and explosives detection.

Index

Picture Credits

About the Author

Gail B. Stewart is the author of more than 240 books for children and teens. She is the mother of three grown sons and lives with her husband in Minneapolis.